RENEW ME

Lindy;

    God Bless you Always.

PSal: 27

    with love

        Blanno

RENEW ME

David Greco

CREATION
HOUSE
Orlando, FL

RENEW ME by David Greco
Published by Creation House
Strang Communications Company
600 Rinehart Road
Lake Mary, Florida 32746
Web site: http://www.creationhouse.com

Unless otherwise noted, all Scripture quotations are from the Holy Bible,
New International Version. Copyright © 1973, 1978, 1984, International
Bible Society. Used by permission.

Scripture quotations marked KJV are from
the King James Version of the Bible.

Scripture quotations marked NKJV are from the
New King James Version of the Bible. Copyright © 1979, 1980,
1982 by Thomas Nelson, Inc., publishers. Used by permission.

Translated by Silvia Cudich

This book was previously published as *Renuévame* by Betania,
un sello de Editorial Caribe, © 1995. ISBN: 0-88113-380-9

Library of Congress Cataloging-in-Publication Data

Greco, David.
Renew me / David Greco.
p.   cm.
ISBN: 0-88419-571-6
1.   Spiritual life—Christianitiy.   I.   Title
BV4501.2.G735   1998   98-29876
243—dc21   CIP

89012345 BBG 87654321

Printed in the United States of America

DEDICATED...

To my late paternal grandmother, Vicenta de Greco—powerful woman of God, woman of sufferings, victorious one.

To my late maternal grandfather, Onofrio Soldano—meek man of God, faithful one who knew how to sow in the kingdom of heaven.

ACKNOWLEDGMENTS

- To my parents, Giacomo and Anna, and to my brother, Ruben, for their sacrifice, vision, work, and unconditional love.

- To my wife, Denise, for her love, her integrity, and her patience.

- To my daughters, Anafaye and Christi, and to my little son, David, for their joy and authentic love.

- To Sheila Greco, for her care and zeal in this project.

- To Pastor Benny Hinn, for his example.

TABLE OF CONTENTS

FOREWORD. viii
PREFACE. x

One
Raised in the Church 1

Two
Wildfire Ignites 16

Three
On the Altar of Sacrifice. 28

Four
Selah. 41

Five
In the Desert of the Spirit 53

Six
Disciple Instead of Follower 66

Seven
According to God's Heart. 87

Eight
In Communion With the Heart of God 111

Nine
Praise That Prevails 133

Ten
The Power of Revelation. 156

Eleven
The Ministry: The Fragrance of Christ. 172

Twelve
The Latter Glory. 192

Thirteen
Open Heavens 213

FOREWORD

AVID GRECO IS an ambassador for the Lord—one whose heart reflects the love of Jesus Christ. One who has been renewed.

David reached the place where he cried out to God, "Renew me!" When a crisis occurred in the home of a friend, even though he had grown up in a Pentecostal home and attended Bible college and seminary, David realized that he had nothing to offer his friend other than powerless words. It was time for renewal. And God renewed him.

The dictionary defines *renew* as "to recover (strength, youth, etc.); to restore to a former state." The Old Testament writer of the Book of Lamentations cries out, "Restore us to yourself, O LORD, that we may return; renew our days as of old" (Lam. 5:21). These words are as applicable today as when they were penned thousands of years ago.

In order for renewal to occur in us, we must first come to the place where we acknowledge that the void inside us cannot be filled by doing all the right things and saying all the right phrases—the routine acts Christians do daily by rote. In the preface to this book, David states, "Renewal happens when a believer surrenders to a 'stripping' process in which the layers of artifice are removed, leaving the exposed individual ready to be recovered, restored, and renewed in the good and perfect will of God." And sometimes that stripping process is painful.

In *Renew Me,* David Greco uses the life of Abraham to guide us on the path to renewal. He helps us see that the wilderness—our most desperate times in our walk with God—brings the power of God. The truths about renewal that David shares in this book will enlighten, inspire, and enrich your relationship with our Savior, the Lord Jesus Christ.

David is a dear friend of mine, someone whose life and ministry are deeply touching the body of Christ. The Lord has given David such a way of ministering the Word of God. He is an anointed and brilliant Bible teacher, and he makes the Word of God come alive in your heart. Every time that I have sat with this man of God, my heart has been stirred.

As you read *Renew Me,* I pray that your heart will also be stirred. We have a promise from our Savior, "Blessed are those who hunger and thirst for righteousness, for they will be filled" (Matt. 5:6). Let us allow the Holy Spirit to renew us—stripping away all that is not of Christ and filling us with more of Christ—and let us then mount up with the wings of eagles and show our world the reality of Jesus Christ.

—PASTOR SAM HINN
THE GATHERING PLACE
LAKE MARY, FLORIDA

PREFACE

REDEMPTION DEALS WITH our sin debt. But the transformation of our attitudes and actions is a process that can be compared roughly to the restoration of a beautiful piece of furniture that has, through the years, been covered with several coats of paint. Over time, every one of us has acquired, to a greater or lesser degree, the world's patterns of thinking and doing things. Sadly, even someone raised in the church—as I was—can adopt the use of artificial coverings designed to project an image or mask flaws. These "protective coatings" actually cause us to become less and less sensitive to God. But God's desire is clear. He wants us to have a constant, vibrant, renewed relationship with Him, full of wonder and surprises.

> Do not conform any longer to the pattern of this world,
> but be transformed by the renewing of your mind.
> Then you will be able to test and approve what God's
> will is—his good, pleasing and perfect will.
> —ROMANS 12:2

World in this verse is translated from the word *cosmos*, from which is also derived the word *cosmetics*. After years of masking ourselves according to the "pattern of this world," we may find that God's original, which He wanted to finish according to His design, has been painted over in such a fashion that it is barely recognizable as His handiwork.

Renewal happens when a believer surrenders to a "stripping" process in which the layers of artifice are removed, leaving the exposed individual ready to be recovered, restored, and renewed in the good and perfect will of God.

I grew up in a Christian home and dedicated my life to serving God at a very early age. I did all that I was taught to do—pray, read the Bible, serve, and sing in church—until it became routine.

As an adult, I became the director of a large ministry that was reaching millions of people. After many years of fruitful service, I found myself in a desert. Opposition arose. Church leaders leveled false accusations against me and my ministry. I was in a spiritual crisis. I looked for support in my church background and seminary training and found that they wouldn't sustain me. Whenever I sought advice, I would hear the same thing: Pray and fast, get into the Word, praise the Lord, and "Greater is He that is in you than he that is in the world...." I became insensitive. I found no delight when I prayed. I merely told God all my sorrows and gave Him my list of needs. I confess I prayed only because I felt I had to; I was afraid God would punish me if I didn't.

During those desperate months, God took me to a new place. I had to leave the old, the habitual, and the familiar behind. I had to hand over to God my self, my reputation, my goals, and my anxieties. It was very hard to give Him my ministry. He had given it to me, and now He was requesting it back. I had to tell the Lord I was willing to be a car salesman or an office employee if necessary.

Layer by layer, I was being renewed. It wasn't an easy process. Over several months, God did a complete stripping of my old ways until I was ready to accept the new. It was then that the Holy Spirit could make real changes.

The first touch of His refinishing brush came one night in Toronto. During a crusade led by a great man of God, the presence of the Holy Spirit manifested in a tangible way in my life. In just a few minutes, the heart that had taken so long to become empty was filled with the glory of God. I had never experienced anything like that in my life. Back home, everything I used to do by rote changed. My quiet times were now vibrant. The Holy Spirit was now real and alive. He enlightened my thoughts. He put in me the desire to pray. He explained biblical truths to me that I had never known before. I began reading old devotional books that lay forgotten in the library, and I spent time listening to worship music. All these things helped me to stay in communion with God.

I began to regard fellow believers in a new light. I was able to perceive in them the fragrance of intimate and loving relationships with God. What had seemed to be purely emotional, immature, simple, or mystic I now saw as a passionate response to God. I longed to express my love to God with such passion.

The most surprising thing was the effect this change had on my ministry. I wanted to pray for those in need. When I did, those I prayed for felt the same glorious presence I was feeling. Many fell to the floor. Others wept. My motivation was no longer just to preach another sermon or simply present the truth of the Word of God. The Holy Spirit was filling me with the desire to see transformed people coming into a new relationship of trust with God.

I would like to be able to say from that moment on everything went well, but it didn't. Many people were uncomfortable with the change in me. But I, like the apostle Paul, "consider everything a loss compared to the surpassing greatness of knowing Christ Jesus my Lord, for whose sake I have lost all things. I consider them rubbish, that I may gain Christ" (Phil. 3:8).

Well-intentioned believers who have appointed themselves as guards against false doctrine surround us. Whenever someone starts to speak about renewal, the "vigilantes" appear. Their zeal leads them to make sure that nothing is "carnal" and everything is according to the established doctrines of the church. I understand. I used to be like that.

In the last few years, I have spoken with many sincere people who have expressed their need for renewal. I have read many books written on this topic; some of them tend to produce guilt feelings and a sense that God is very disappointed in us. Let me assure you I will not be doing that in this book.

My prayer is that through this book your spiritual life will be transformed by the power of the Holy Spirit. If you are going through a desert of dissatisfaction and frustration, be encouraged! You are a candidate for renewal. God wants to lead you to a new place. Wait for Him. This promise is ours:

> Do you not know?
>   Have you not heard?
> The LORD is the everlasting God,
>   the Creator of the ends of the earth.
> He will not grow tired or weary,
>   and his understanding no one can fathom.
> He gives strength to the weary
>   and increases the power of the weak.
> Even youths grow tired and weary,
>   and young men stumble and fall;
> but those who hope in the LORD
>   will renew their strength.
> They will soar on wings like eagles;
>   they will run and not grow weary,
>   they will walk and not be faint.
>   —ISAIAH 40:28–31

The eagle's beak is sharp and shaped like a hook. This allows the eagle to defend itself, kill its prey, and eat. To keep his beak from growing so much that it crooks to the point where the eagle can't open it anymore, the bird looks for a rough rock against which to rub its beak to maintain its original shape—constantly renewing its shape.

This is God's promise: If you feel weary and tired, He doesn't. If your Christian life has become a burden and you can't rejoice in Christ, God wants to renew you, sanding down all those things that stop you from feeling the freshness of His glorious and life-giving presence. Those who faint, who feel weary and tired, with no strength left in them, those who have stumbled, and even fallen, are candidates for renewal. And those who wait and trust that God will give them new strength will be renewed!

One

RAISED IN THE CHURCH

I HAD JUST FINISHED seminary and was looking forward to beginning a doctoral program at Temple University. After four years of Bible college and two years in seminary, my long-held dream of becoming a doctor of theology was just materializing. Then, abruptly, it was shattered with a single phone call.

I stood, without a word, in the kitchen of the Pennsylvania apartment where I lived with my wife, Denise, during our school years. I held the phone to my ear and just listened as a college friend, a pastor's son with whom I had played in a Christian music group, poured out his heart to me from the other end of the line.

He was in tears. He said that his wife had left him and was going to start divorce proceedings. He wanted my advice. Our families back in New York were friends. He had been in my wedding party. As he sobbed into the telephone, I was deeply moved and wanted to help.

My emotions pounded away at me, insisting that with my exemplary Christian upbringing and advanced seminary training, I must have answers for my friend. I kept listening while I made a frantic mental search of my background and struggled to come up with the right words.

I had been born a fourth-generation evangelical on my father's side and a third-generation one on my mother's. My parents instilled in me love and respect for the church and the pastors, elders, and leaders in authority over us. My parents and my uncle modeled diligent servanthood, taking on a number of roles in the church—board member, choir leader, and eldership. My grandparents were models of persistent faithfulness that spanned decades.

As a small boy, I was fascinated by everything that took place in church. I liked the microphones and music, the preachers and pulpits, the baptismal and communion services, and any other activity the church could organize. By age two, I was already showing an inclination toward preaching. By age seven and a half, I responded to God's call and dedicated my future to His service. I was sure God would use me as a pastor, preacher, and certainly a musician since I had a deep attraction to musical instruments.

I did everything I could in my young life to learn the lessons of the local church "laboratory." I had my mischievous moments, but I learned to act like a Christian according to the rules and regulations of the church. The rules were relatively simple: As boys, we were expected to wear a shirt, a tie, and a jacket. Our hair had to be short, and we were supposed to be at every service and activity of the church. We couldn't go to the beach, dances, parties, or any other entertainment.

The rules for the girls were even stricter. Elders in the church were placed in charge of making sure that these rules were strictly applied, standing as guards at the church door. When one was accepted, the rewards were being allowed to participate in the church's activities, possibly being given some official position, and being considered "a good boy or girl."

Later in life I would thank God for the protection that came with the restrictions imposed on me. But the problem with all those rules lay in the fact that they were presented as a pattern for holiness, and their violation was considered sin.

Holiness—serving God, "being on good terms" with God, being in the center of His will—was reduced to the act of following the regulations of the church to the letter.

My family never taught me that breaking the rules was sin. They simply explained to me that we had to be an example to other families in the church. But as a child, and later as a young man, I couldn't understand their reasoning.

In 1966 the fashion style changed. Men's pants were very wide at the hemlines and were known as "bell bottoms." My brother and I convinced my mother to allow us to buy new pants so we would not have to wear our narrow ones. My mother had no objections, and my brother bought a pair of white pants. That weekend when our pastor saw him, he was threatened with disciplinary measures—to be fashionably dressed was sin; going against fashion was a sign of holiness. Message after message was given from the pulpit against the fashions of the world.

"I'M SITTING ON THE OUTSIDE, BUT INSIDE I'M STANDING UP"

I LOVED MUSIC, and in order to maintain my position as a musician in the church, I obeyed the established regulations. But I wasn't doing it from my heart; I was obedient because it was in my own interest. There is a story about a mischievous little boy whose mother decides to punish him by having him sit on a chair for a long time. After a few seconds, the boy says, "I'm sitting on the outside, but inside I'm standing up."

That was me, outwardly obedient to what was requested of me but disobedient in my heart. I pretended to be a good young Christian. In spite of my impure heart, God blessed me and poured His grace on my life. Deep inside, I knew that one day I was going to have to be honest with God. The "religious" games eventually would have to come to an end.

3

CHRISTIAN ARTIST

IN 1971 WE left Argentina and went to live in New York City. At my parents' urging, I went to the city's public university. But I wasn't too sure of the direction in which I was heading.

One day a friend invited me to become the pianist in a Christian musical group. The members of this group were young men who were full of enthusiasm and big plans. Our goal was fame. I thought this was the perfect opportunity to fulfill God's calling on my life and, at the same time, do something that I deeply loved: be a musician.

We would sing and testify in churches, concerts, and open air meetings. After some weeks, the group director realized that I could preach better than the others, so he put me in charge of the preaching at the end of our musical programs. The message was always the same: "Everything goes well with Christ. Believe in Him, and everything will be all right."

One Saturday evening we performed in a big concert. The promoter had contracted us to open for a very famous music group. We were delighted. We were reaching our goal, gaining notoriety. After a particular moving song, I said a few challenging words to the audience. I saw some in the crowd wiping tears from their eyes.

As soon as we were off the platform, the promoter called us over. He was very upset. He said that although we had sung very well, the people had been depressed by the short inspirational message. He said no one should preach during a concert—just sing. He said that if we wanted to succeed, we couldn't challenge the public with uncomfortable messages.

Even when I did preach, I began to realize that the entertaining, inspirational message I delivered was not what people needed to hear. They were hungry for God, for something real. But I had nothing to give them. At the end of the concerts they would congratulate us for our dedication and for the anointing they perceived upon our ministry. They thought we had a wonderful relationship with God.

They were so deceived! In reality, we were a group of hungry, needy people, challenging others who were also hungry and needy.

ON TO BIBLE SCHOOL!

I REMEMBER THE morning I realized how frustrated I was—frustrated with school, with God's calling, with the musical group, and with the course my life was taking. One of the singers in my group told me he felt the same way. We decided that the solution to our problems was to study in our denomination's Christian college in Pennsylvania. After convincing the rest of our group, we all enrolled in Valley Forge Christian College, a Christian school with special programs for people training for a career in ministry.

What a surprise Christian college was for me! For the very first time in my life I felt the strong tug of temptation. For the very first time I was away from my parents' supervision and the close watch of the brothers in my local church. Since I was boarding at the school, I had to sleep alone, administer my time, and choose my new friends. In many of my classes, the professors belittled most of the ideas I had learned in church, calling them "Sunday school theology" and promising to bring further enlightenment to me.

I stayed there for four years. I learned to question everything I heard about God or read in the Bible. I was taught to examine everything, to be suspicious of anything that could be attributed to "experience and emotions."

Among the students were some serious young men who I thought had their heads in the clouds. Always well dressed, these young men prayed, prophesied, and participated in all the "spiritual" activities in the school. I would mock them, calling them "little preachers." I was more interested in being popular. I wanted to be considered nice, funny, and intellectual. Spiritual and mystical? Never!

My teachers instilled in me a true passion for studying and acquiring knowledge. Passion for knowledge produces even more passion for knowledge. This can easily become pride, which is exactly what happened to me. When I heard a pastor preaching, I criticized all the hermeneutic mistakes he was making. I laughed at all the "simple things" I heard from the pulpit.

Every week I ministered to others with a group of students. One of my responsibilities was to preach. My messages were ideas and concepts received from my teachers and my own academic research. I repeated what others had experienced. I loved to interpret biblical passages from the translation of words and phrases in their original languages. I loved to read theological material, biblical commentaries, and analytical studies. I hated devotional books; they were boring. My goal was to acquire great knowledge, which would give me credibility, recognition, and a good reputation.

When preaching, my heart would fill with pride as I insinuated that my exposition was the *right* interpretation of the Bible passage. I thought other preachers didn't know as much as I did. Even though I didn't verbalize my feelings of superiority, every time I stood before a congregation I clearly projected those feelings to the listeners.

During my last year of college, I met my wife, Denise, a girl brought up in a good Christian home. She constantly tried to help me become aware of my problem with spiritual pride, but I did not want to accept that truth. I didn't think *I* had a problem; *the others* did.

My vision had changed. My focus no longer was to announce to the world that Jesus Christ was the only hope for eternal life. I wanted to impress people with my theological knowledge. My ambition was to correct all the doctrinal and theological mistakes in the church.

Deep inside of me, though, I envied simple Christianity. I remember wanting to be like Yiye Avila, the famous Puerto

Rican evangelist. It seemed to me that he had no theological education—just a simple heart message. In moments of difficult financial situations, loneliness, and sickness, I wanted to have the very simple faith I despised. I remembered my own family members. My grandmother Vicenta was a woman of prayer and faith. My grandfather Onofrio was a man of prayer and was totally dedicated to the study of the Bible. They had something I coveted—they knew God intimately. My grandmother and grandfather were friends of God.

I recalled that when my brother and I were sick, my parents would call the elders of the church. Brother Horacio, a deacon in our church, would come to our house during his lunch break to pray with my grandmother and mother for our healing. Even though they didn't know much academically, they knew God. When they prayed, God answered; Jesus' healing power touched us time after time.

After finishing my bachelor's degree in theology, I decided to go to seminary. I wanted to get a doctorate in theology from one of the most important universities in the country. I studied about God, history, and the development of Christian thought and psychology under the best Catholic and Protestant teachers of contemporary theology.

At seminary, I learned to be even more critical of the "simplicity of the gospel." I learned that spiritual truths were complicated and difficult to understand. I could only interpret certain truths through study. My teachers taught me that biblical concepts are wrapped in culture, language, and historical context. My responsibility was to "unwrap" those truths so I could interpret and understand them in the context of our culture.

During those years at seminary, I rose to a new level of pride and frustration. I came to the conclusion that everybody was wrong. I convinced myself that the church needed a radical change in its biblical teachings, and I was one of the people who were going to bring about this change. What a fantasy!

These high and lofty thoughts were toppled by that afternoon call from my friend. With all my upbringing and all my training, all I could think of to tell this hurting brother was that he should look for a professional counselor trained in these matters. I felt terrible. All my friend needed was a word of encouragement and comfort, and I had failed.

After a few days, he called me again to let me know that Rev. Kenneth Griepp, a dear friend of ours, was going to be his counselor. I tried to convince him otherwise, thinking a pastor could not help him. But he insisted, so I went to New York to talk to Pastor Griepp, planning to scrutinize his counseling methods.

After listening to my academic ideas, Pastor Griepp told me, "The weapons we fight with are not the weapons of the world . . . They have divine power to demolish strongholds. We demolish arguments and every pretension that sets itself up against the knowledge of God, and we take captive every thought to make it obedient to Christ."

His words had an impact on me. Where did he get them? I started to make a list in my mind of all the books where he could have found such powerful words.

Back at home, I searched my library in vain. Suddenly, I had a terrifying thought: *Could it be a Bible verse?* It sounded familiar. I ran to my concordance, and there I found it. The pastor had quoted from 2 Corinthians 10:4–5. I felt ashamed. After years of theological studies, I hadn't even recognized a Bible verse. How was it possible, since I had read the Bible cover to cover so many times? Even worse, I remembered that I had taken a semester's study of 1 and 2 Corinthians.

After several minutes, I made a decision to forget the pursuit of a doctorate. What I had learned was of no use to me. I hadn't been able to help my friend. My mind was saturated with knowledge, theory, and concepts—none of which I could use in a time of real crisis. I was disturbed because I was so unfamiliar with the Bible. My mind was saturated with concepts—not with the living Word of God.

Much is said today about spiritual warfare and struggles against principalities and powers. People are very interested in knowing about the schemes of the enemy, demonic strategies, and other horrifying details. So many Christians are more interested in discerning the names and ranks of rulers, authorities, powers, and spiritual forces than in knowing the wonderful names of God that represent the different aspects of His glorious character. More literature is written and more seminars are given on demonology than on Christology. We are so worried about the external struggle that Satan is able to distract us from the battlefields that are most important for growth and maturity: our own minds.

The spiritual warfare in which I found myself engaged was not taking place in a city or a territory or a project or a vision; it was taking place in my mind. Note what Paul says:

> The weapons we fight with are not the weapons of the world. On the contrary, they have divine power to demolish strongholds. We demolish arguments and every pretension that sets itself up against the knowledge of God, and we take captive every thought to make it obedient to Christ.
>
> —2 CORINTHIANS 10:4–5

There are several key words in these verses that we are not used to using in everyday language. Yet they come into play every day as we battle to keep our thoughts focused on Jesus Christ.

1. Stronghold

What is a *stronghold?* It is "a castle, a fortified site, a well-defended place" that inspires confidence because it is impregnable. We have to demolish such strongholds by refuting arguments and every pretension.

2. Argument

What does the word *argument* mean? My car once had a mechanical problem. I took it to the repair shop, and the mechanic gave me an estimate. I wanted to know the cost of repairing my car. The mechanic was very clear in explaining that the price might vary according to his findings inside the engine. He had only taken an outside look at it. Arguments are like the estimates: We arrive at them because we do not have all the information we need.

An argument, as it is used in this passage, is a conclusion derived from false or inadequate premises. How many assumptions we make about God based on superficial analysis! We say that God acts in such and such a way, sees the situation in this or that way, or looks for certain things in our lives. But the majority of these conclusions do not reflect the real heart of God.

Satan is expert at presenting false claims about God. That is exactly what he did with Eve in the Garden of Eden and with Jesus in the desert. He presented "arguments." They appear to come from God, and they even sound like God, but they are not authentic.

Where do these arguments germinate? In the mind.

3. Pretension

What is a *pretension?* It's "something elevated, something that rises against, in opposition." When I was young, I loved to run away from the service to be with my little friends from church. The best time to do this was at the end of the message when my dad was busy counting the offering and my mom and the rest of the congregation were praying with their eyes closed. That was the opportune time for the children. But our greatest obstacles were the deacons that served as doormen. These doormen were our "barriers." They were our opposition—and they were much taller and smarter than we were.

A barrier gets in the way because it is difficult to go through it. Second Corinthians 10:5 says the "pretension" or barrier sets itself up against the knowledge of God. It doesn't allow us to know Him as a person or to develop an intimate relationship with Him.

Where are these barriers? Where is the pretension that exalts itself against the knowledge of God erected? In the mind.

4. Thought

Paul concludes by saying that we need to take captive every thought to make it obedient to Christ. A *thought* is "an intellectual perception, an opinion that is formed after an analysis." We analyze the deeds of others and rapidly formulate our own opinions about them. When we accumulate enough opinions, we have an impregnable stronghold. Nobody will be able to change our convictions. We have arrived at an inflexible conclusion. Where do these thoughts reside? Where do these opinions abide? In the mind. My mind was saturated with arguments, pretensions, and thoughts, which had become a stronghold.

A *stronghold,* then, is a castle made out of *arguments.* It's a fortified place not made with bricks or mortar or cement, but with *pretensions.* It's a barrier composed of *thoughts* and opinions that oppose the true and legitimate knowledge of God. It is a house built with erroneous thoughts. This stronghold controls our mind and our behavior.

When the Word of God proclaimed by Pastor Griepp tried to penetrate my mind, there was a collision against my intellectual and religious strongholds. My problem wasn't a conflict with principalities, demons, or powers; my main problem was the strongholds that did not allow me to know God intimately. Even though I knew a lot about Him, my being didn't know the living God. I didn't experience the longing King David did to behold His power and His glory. (See Psalm 63:1–2.)

I believe demonic beings exist. But I believe their principal strategy is to find Christians who have strongholds in their minds. When they find them, they find a place, a territory where they can live and work. Paul tells us clearly that we can't give the devil a "foothold." What are these "footholds"? They are the strongholds, arguments, pretensions, and thoughts in our minds.

A RADICAL CHANGE OF ATTITUDE

I RECOGNIZED I had no intimate relationship with God. I threw away all my books, diplomas, and certificates. I thought I knew a lot and was ready to serve God in the ministry, but that day I realized I needed a change in my spiritual life. I was lost. I knew I was hungry, but I didn't know how to get food. My soul was thirsty, but I didn't know how to reach the spring of water. I needed an answer, but I didn't know where to find it.

My situation was critical. I had already finished my studies. I had been offered several ministry positions. I was at a crossroad. I had to decide what to do with my life. Was I prepared for the ministry? Those who knew me thought I was.

But I was in anguish. For years I had trusted my knowledge and talents, the strength of my character, my testimony, and my family. I had a clean past, good academic training, and a calling to the ministry. But I felt incapable of ministering to others.

I watched my school friends who were already in ministry. I could see a real enthusiasm in some of them, but most were disappointed. The ministry was not what they had expected. Generally I would hear complaints. Was that going to be my future? My wife and I decided to go back to New York to live with my parents. I thought that if God needed me, He would know where to find me.

When I got home, I immediately went to see Pastor Griepp, who was then the assistant pastor at Gateway Cathedral in Staten Island, New York. He was already counseling my friend. Again I tried to impress him with my knowledge, but I couldn't. He had already gone through that "intellectual" stage in his own life. He told me I needed a change in my life. His advice was to forget my career in ministry. I felt attacked, wounded, and despised. He had hit a raw nerve, and it hurt.

I knew my only solution was to sit in church and be discipled by a pastor who would teach me how to serve God from the heart. After talking to Rev. Daniel Mercaldo, the senior pastor of Gateway Cathedral, we decided to stay in New York and become a part of his congregation.

We had come back without much hope. After many years of studying, I had terrible debts. My wife and I would have to work for years to pay off those debts. After all my theological training and ministry experiences, I ended up living with my parents, in debt, and without a ministry position.

We became a part of Gateway. There the Lord sat me down in a church pew to receive real practical spiritual training. Through my pastor I received a truly biblical education. His preaching and teaching showed me that I needed to know the Word of God in a different way from what I had been taught in the seminary.

I had learned to study the Word of God in a scientific way, following rules of hermeneutic interpretation. My teachers had taught me the goal was to arrive at the truth— not to change or be transformed. But in service after service, meeting after meeting, talk after talk, I perceived my pastor's main purpose was not simply to teach the truth. His deep desire was that the truth would *produce a change* in the lives of those listening.

As I made friends with those in the congregation, I saw the truth enabling men and women to change their attitudes, behaviors, family lives, devotional lives, goals, habits, and plans. I felt ashamed as I realized new converts knew God more intimately than I did.

The contact with these new Christians who had been revolutionized by Jesus Christ produced a deep hunger in me.

I longed to have a simple and plain relationship with God as they did. I was tired of reading my Bible as if it were a technical manual; I was tired of asking for His direction of my career in ministry and presenting to Him my needs. I was tired of thinking God was a taskmaster who is waiting for us to pay Him back with our work. There was no joy in my relationship with Him. I needed to be renewed.

Can you identify with my situation? Many Christians have lost their initial enthusiasm. Many believers are comfortable with their Christianity. They go to church, minister, give offerings, and are good witnesses—but that's all. They don't have anything new to give. There is no new experience, no freshness in their relationship with God. When they arrive at church, their only concerns are what is being done, how it is being done, and who is doing it. On the other hand, new Christians smile, sing, hug one another, and give simple and childlike testimonies. They are filled with thanksgiving, joy, and enthusiasm. Perhaps you—a comfortable believer who has seen it all—smile and say that eventually they will change and become "normal" like you.

However, in the depth of your heart, do you desire to be like them? Admit it. Be honest. Don't be satisfied with your growth or your stable spiritual life; don't become comfortable. Recognize your frustration. If you continue on this path, nothing will ever change. Confess that you need a change. Don't be proud and adopt a defensive attitude. God has new and wonderful things that will renew your spiritual life.

> Do not conform any longer to the pattern of this world, but be transformed by the renewing of your mind. Then you will be able to test and approve what God's will is—his good, pleasing and perfect will.
>
> —ROMANS 12:2

In the Bible, God opens His heart to us, revealing the kind of people He wants us to be. Through the examples of biblical men and women, God gives us patterns to follow and encourages us to seek the same experiences, to develop the same character, and to obtain the same knowledge. But there is a huge distance between reality and that goal.

We are bogged down in evaluating success and victory—even in our churches—according to standards set up by the world.

God wants us to be renewed in our understanding so we won't walk according to the ideas of the world; we will walk according to what is pleasing to Him, according to what is perfect. If you live in this twentieth-century society, the world and its culture have powerfully affected you. God wants to renew you so that your mind, your heart, and your life may be guided by His will. In order to achieve this, God will allow you to go through a difficult process, but it is worthwhile. Through these pages I will try to share some of the procedures God uses to renew us.

Two

WILDFIRE IGNITES

WHEN I FINISHED school, a commercial radio station offered me an administrative job, which I accepted after returning to New York. There I met a group of believers who were buying weekly airtime with that station for the preaching of the gospel. After a few months, they began to have financial difficulties and couldn't afford the fee the radio station demanded.

Although they tried to continue with their weekly program, after a year they told me they had to abandon the project due to lack of funds. I suggested they go on the air one last time, informing the listeners that unless they received voluntary offerings for the support of the radio program, that Saturday broadcast would be their last.

The appeal was successful, and listeners made commitments to send offerings to cover the monthly cost of the airtime. We decided to expand by buying more hours for the spreading and preaching of the Word of God—and thus, Radio Vision Cristiana (Radio Vision) was born.

At that time we didn't know the plans that God had for this ministry. After a few months, I resigned from my administrative job at the radio station to become executive director for Radio Vision, a position I still hold today.

Radio Vision's first official broadcast was on April 7, 1984. It covered the entire metropolitan area of New York City, which has a population of twenty million, four million of whom are Hispanic. We continued to buy more and more airtime, until we were broadcasting fourteen hours a day. Then we decided to purchase the radio station over which we were broadcasting. The last day of June 1989, Radio Vision purchased WNYM for thirteen million dollars. July 1, 1989, WWRV went out over the airwaves as the first Hispanic Christian radio station in New York City. It had a purely noncommercial format, and to this day it remains entirely listener supported.

God's people continued to cover all the station's expenses with monthly offerings of five, ten, and twenty dollars. Three years after seeing God's powerful hand at work in the initial purchase of WWRV, the Hispanic evangelical community, the church leaders on the Radio Vision Board of Directors, and those of us on the executive staff were filled with an expectant joy. The construction of our second station was nearly complete, and it would soon be ready to go on the air. It was going to be international in scope, reaching twenty million listeners in the Caribbean and in Central and South America.

The events leading up to the purchase of this second radio station were miraculous. While attending the annual Christian communications convention in Washington, D.C., a man approached me, offering to sell me a radio station on an unknown island in the Caribbean. This man, a businessperson from the South, tried to convince me by saying that this radio station could reach Cuba. The price was two and a half million dollars. I told him that even though the offer was tempting, the price was too high.

Some months went by. Our then president, Rev. Luciano Padilla, Jr. (a man with great vision), attended a leaders' conference in Virginia. While he was there, the new owners of that radio station offered it to Reverend Padilla since they weren't making any money with it. The price had gone down to a million dollars. We still thought it was too high.

After several months, the owners called to ask me how much we could offer for it. They accepted my offer to purchase the Caribbean radio station for three hundred twenty-five thousand dollars.

The station was located on a British island about two hundred miles from Cuba, one hundred twenty miles north of the Dominican Republic, and four hundred miles northwest of Puerto Rico. The broadcasting lines from our studios in Paterson, New Jersey, to the satellite plant were already in place. The signal to the satellite located twenty-two thousand feet in space was going to be launched live. From there, it would be rebroadcast to our new international radio station. This signal would fly through the Caribbean and the rest of Latin America with one hundred thousand watts of power.

There were many reasons to rejoice. God was handing us a huge platform from which to announce the good news of salvation to a part of our continent that was, and still is, suffering under poverty, dictatorships, and demonic Afro-Indian sects.

I had some anxious thoughts. Since the beginning of 1984, through the proclamation of the simple gospel of Christ, thousands had been saved. However, I felt that what we had been doing was not going to be enough. We needed something new and different for this international radio opportunity.

Have you ever felt that your life needs to be revitalized? Many feel uncomfortable with this truth. They feel condemned. Many believe that if they need a change it's because what they are doing is wrong. Many reject the idea of renewal because they think they have to admit that their Christian lives have been failures. No! There comes a time when the Holy Spirit will introduce us to experiences where what we have learned in the past is not enough. The Holy Spirit Himself makes us hungry and thirsty for more. This doesn't mean we need to throw away everything we have learned or practiced before. The Holy Spirit wants to introduce us to a new level so we can achieve new purposes in God.

We knew God was doing wonders in Cuba. The church of our Lord was experiencing an incredible growth there. In the Dominican Republic, the church had multiplied six times in the last ten years. The church in Central America is huge. In some countries like Guatemala, 50 percent of the population is evangelical. God was giving us the privilege of reaching Cuba, the Dominican Republic, Puerto Rico, and parts of Central and South America from our radio station via satellite, without ever leaving New York City.

The construction of the station and acquisition of the necessary licenses had cost over a million dollars. Radio Vision was a ministry supported entirely by the voluntary offerings of our Hispanic Christian radio audience and supporters. We never sold programs or commercial advertising. All the money to complete this project had been supplied by generous Christians from New York and New Jersey. The Christian family was overjoyed. They had given their money so their relatives in their countries of origin could listen to the message of Christ. They had good reasons to rejoice. We were fulfilling the Great Commission.

But what did we, the church in New York, have to say? What was our message? Was it to be the same as always? The same routine, the same experiences, and the same clichés? We had to express something new, something fresh.

We had raised the money for the radio station in "radio marathons." These special programs, which include preaching and prayer, raise money for the support of the ministry from our listeners. Although our people were extremely generous, the radio marathons were tiring. There were times when these fundraisers would last up to two months. This worried me. *If we keep asking the people for money,* I thought, *they are going to get tired and stop giving.* The expense of putting an international radio station on the

19

air was going to be astronomical. We needed something different. Unfortunately, I didn't know where to find that something different.

The Storm

During the next few months, through His people God gave us all the money we needed to build the new radio station. Things were going well. The enthusiasm was contagious. The funds had arrived. Everything was wonderful.

But suddenly, a series of wildfires ignited. A group of people started to spread false accusations against us, saying that the international radio station project was a fraud. According to them, the money raised to buy and build the station was being used for our own personal gain. We were branded as thieves.

These false accusations caused a lot of harm. A large number of faithful supporters, among them several church leaders, believed these slanderous rumors. Many fomented distrust. We started to receive letters from lawyers threatening to bring us to a press conference to be unmasked. Ministers met together to accuse Radio Vision of fraud and deception.

We prayed, "Lord, free us! Get us out of this! Defend us!" Tears would flow as our desperate clamor rose.

We felt that God was constantly saying to us, "Don't be afraid, and don't defend yourselves; I'm working." Of course, that's easy to say when everything is going well. However, when there are slanderers and malicious people, when accusations stain our reputations and the whole vision is in danger, it isn't so easy. My life revolved around the ministry. If the ministry collapsed, so would my life.

We went through terribly anxious moments. The uncertainty was overwhelming. What would happen if the people, the pastors, and the supporters stopped helping us? If those offerings didn't come, the ministry would die. The radio station in New York had to produce monthly funds in order to pay for the bank loan and the general expenses incurred with a staff of forty-six employees. Our annual budget exceeded four million dollars.

I could feel this burden resting on my shoulders. I was controlled by negative thoughts. I had no strength left. When I prayed, the words would not come out of my mouth. I had no more tears. I had never felt like that. I had always been able to find a solution, an idea, a way out. However, not this time.

On top of all this, I was hiding the details of the approaching danger from my colleagues and the Board of Directors. My wife was asking questions; my family wanted to know what was going on. The radio programmers wanted more information about the accusations.

We planned strategies to counteract the slander; none of them worked. The accusers grew stronger every passing day. I complained to the Lord, spending hours explaining to Him what was going on—as if He didn't know.

What else could I do? I was simply doing what I had been taught to do: Cry out to the Lord. For me, crying out to the Lord was presenting my need, explaining my pain, and shedding tears before a merciful God. I thought my pain would move God's hand on our behalf.

Many believe they can move God by simply crying or expressing their pain. No! The Bible says it clearly. Even though God has compassion for us, only one thing moves His heart. It isn't my need. It isn't my trouble. It isn't how serious the situation is or how desperate I am. *It is faith.* Without faith, it is impossible to please God.

I wasn't showing much faith as I spent hours prostrate on the floor or lying on the couch, telling God my troubles. I was simply unloading my sorrows, my burdens, and my worries. If you are going through a desperate situation, don't think God will feel sorry for you. God loves you; however, He doesn't feel sorry for His children. In the midst of an impossible situation, He wants us to trust in Him.

In Matthew 15 and Mark 7, we find the story of the

Syrophoenician woman. This woman had a serious problem: Her daughter had an evil spirit. Put yourself in the place of this mother who constantly witnessed the demon afflicting her daughter. Nobody could do anything for her. Neither science nor religion could heal her. That woman—who wasn't a Jew, but a Gentile—heard that Jesus, a Jewish rabbi, cast out evil spirits. Immediately she decided to meet with the Master.

Mark 7:24 says that Jesus went to the region of Tyre, a gentile nation, to hide from the crowd and from the Pharisees who were constantly after Him. Yet He couldn't hide from this woman. She came before Him and fell at His feet. What reverence! What fear! She was a desperate woman. She thought that if she revered Jesus, surely she would receive the miracle she needed from Him. She not only fell at His feet, but she also began to acknowledge the position and the attributes of Jesus. She started out by calling Him "Lord, Son of David." She recognized that Jesus was the Messiah, God's anointed One. Her petition was simple: "My daughter is suffering terribly from demon possession." The Bible says she was "crying out" with all her might. (See Matthew 15:22.)

Jesus did not answer. He kept silent. His silence was powerful. The silence of God is extremely powerful. God doesn't always answer our petitions immediately, but He listens right away. Then comes the silence. Jesus didn't move; He didn't even seem to react.

The disciples didn't understand Jesus' silence, just as you and I don't understand His silence. When God remains silent in our lives, we rapidly elaborate an argument, an opinion, and a speculation. We think, *God is angry with me. I'm in trouble.* The disciples thought Jesus was pretending not to hear, and they urged Him to send her away. How many times have you presented a need before God and not received an answer? How quickly we are assaulted by thoughts like: *Stop pushing; God is not going to give you an answer. God only answers mature, strong, and special*

Christians. Give up and do something by your own efforts! Yet God remains silent.

So there I was. I prayed and cried out. I complained to God and to my partners in ministry. However, God would not speak. No prophets appeared with a heavenly message, and the situation wasn't getting any better. The heavens were apparently closed, and it felt as if God weren't listening to me.

Jesus responded to His disciples' request to send the woman away by saying that the Messiah, the Son of David, had been sent only to the lost sheep of Israel. Why did Jesus make this clear? Because the woman had acknowledged Him as the Son of David, the Messiah of Israel. The Son of David was not sent to the Gentiles but to the Jews. She had invoked God's covenant with Israel, but the promises of the Old Covenant didn't move Jesus' heart.

The woman didn't give up. This time, calling Him *Lord,* she appealed to His heart, asking for help. In verse 26 of Matthew 15, still talking to His disciples, Jesus says that the bread meant for *children,* meaning the *Jews,* could not be tossed to the *dogs,* meaning the *Gentiles.* What humiliation! The Teacher compared her to a "little dog." Why was Jesus treating this woman so harshly?

She quickly responded, "Yes, Lord, You are right; I can't receive the promises of the Old Covenant with Israel because I'm not Jewish. My desperate need doesn't deserve Your help. But although I'm a little dog, You are my Master! Give me bread!"

Master is equivalent to the word *Lord.* She understood that Jesus, the Giver of life, was absolute Lord; just a few crumbs were sufficient for her. The woman spoke in faith. She didn't appeal to the Old Covenant, her pain, or her need, but to Jesus' sovereignty. And she put her faith in Him.

Jesus, now addressing her for the first time, said, "Woman, you have great faith! Your request is granted" (Matt. 15:28). This woman's faith moved our Lord Jesus.

God seeks faith. While I spent hours asking for help, God

was silent. As I reminded Him that He had to help me because He Himself had called me to this ministry, He still kept silent. However, when I took a step of faith and surrendered myself to His hands, to the hands of the Owner and absolute Lord of my life, He finally spoke.

My first step of faith was to take a one-week vacation. Normally, in the midst of a crisis, we want to stay in the fight, resisting and resolving problems. We think we are important and that God needs us. My wife, realizing I was mentally and physically exhausted, encouraged me to go away.

She didn't know how serious the whole thing was. Just a few moments before I left the office, one of my accusers called and threatened to destroy me. I didn't resist; I started to cry. It was the final accusation—they were going to accuse us in front of the secular press and then take us to court.

HUNGER FOR GOD

I LEFT THE office with my eyes filled with tears. I picked up my family and started driving to Orlando, Florida—a trip that would last twenty-two hours by car. During those long hours as my wife and girls slept, I asked the Lord to speak to me more powerfully than He had ever done before. I determined to go to Pastor Benny Hinn's church that Sunday. I knew God used Pastor Benny in the healing ministry, but this time I asked God to speak to me directly through His servant.

During the entire week we stayed in Orlando, I tried to enjoy my vacation, but I was frequently thinking about my situation in New York. My heart was focused on Benny Hinn's Sunday service, on the service where God was going to speak to me. I was sure that He was going to do something in my life. When Sunday arrived, I was one of the first ones in the sanctuary. I sat in one of the pews at the back; I didn't want anyone to recognize me.

I was hungry; I deeply longed for an answer from God. Only someone who has been desperately hungry can understand this. Mental strongholds fill the heart to such an extent that there is no place for authentic renewal. However, in the midst of a critical situation, God captures our attention. In the midst of a crisis where there is no way out, we look for alternatives. This is where the hunger begins. Renewal begins with the hunger for God—hunger to reach new experiences, new signs, and new insights of God's work in our heart. Because of my pride and my self-sufficiency, I had never developed this desperate hunger. However, through this trial, God was humbling me.

As the service started, I forgot all my problems and was oblivious to those sitting next to me. The worship, the choir, the music, all that was being done, captivated my attention. All I could think of was that God was going to speak to me through His Word. The moment arrived. The pastor opened the Bible and read the biblical passage. The message was based on Genesis 17, where God reminds Abram of the promise of a son and then changes his name from Abram to Abraham, making a final covenant in relationship to the Promised Land.

The central message was that God came to fulfill this promise when Abraham was ninety-nine years old. The pastor concluded by saying that Abraham surrendered completely to God's hands when he reached his old age, when he no longer could do anything in his own strength. In that situation of total physical disability, God revealed Himself as the almighty God, *El Shaddai,* "He who is more than sufficient, He who can satisfy us completely." The message's final challenge was directed to those who were facing an impossible situation like Abraham—old, with a barren wife, and waiting for a son and a miracle.

That was me; I had received a promise, God had called me to serve Him, and I had made a covenant to serve Him for the rest of my life. God had led me step by step with His powerful hand. Since my childhood and youth, He had guarded me from temptations and falls. He had guided me during my school years, and finally He had opened a great ministry, prosperous and full of vision. However, in that moment it seemed everything that God had promised was about to vanish.

The message was for me. God had spoken to me. I had to follow Abraham's example. In the final prayer, I promised God that even though I didn't understand the details, I was going to obey His Word.

That same morning we packed our suitcases and returned to New York. I honestly don't remember much of the trip, even though I was driving. My wife and girls slept most of the way. In those silent hours, the Holy Spirit cut my heart in a thousand pieces with His sword. I felt small, incapable, and ignorant. I felt like a beggar, a man in need, an invalid. This was the work of the Holy Spirit. Although I felt weak, I didn't feel desperate. There was a confidence in me that I couldn't understand. The smaller I felt, the more confident and secure I felt. Confidence in my own knowledge and skills disappeared. My trust in the almighty God, *El Shaddai,* grew. He, only He, could produce a miracle. He, only He, could change my heart and renew me.

When we stopped for food or gas, I grabbed my Bible to read Genesis 17. I realized Abraham's spiritual journey had not started at that moment, but back in his homeland many years before. I decided to study the life of Abraham in detail. God was about to revolutionize my life.

How different are God's ways! How many times we think that He prefers strong, solid, and victorious believers. Apparently God prospers those who try hard, those who are always doing something in the church. Are not these the ones who are constantly testifying about what God is doing in their lives?

My wife and I have two girls and a little boy: Anafaye is thirteen, Christi Joy is ten, and David is four. We love them all the same. However, when one gets sick or doesn't feel well, we devote all our efforts to comfort and take care of that child. Why? Because the son or daughter who is sick needs our attention more than those who are well. If we, being imperfect parents, know how to give good gifts to our children, how much more our Father, who didn't spare His own Son, will protect us and take good care of us. This is not a personal and human revelation; Jesus said it:

> If you, then, though you are evil, know how to give good gifts to your children, how much more will your Father in heaven give good gifts to those who ask him!
> —MATTHEW 7:11

Are you going through a desert of loneliness? Has God promised you something that you haven't received? Are you waiting for God's direction, and it won't come? Is there a threat over your life, over your family, or over your marriage? Are you rejected? Are your talents despised? Do you feel abandoned? Don't despair! The almighty God is about to appear in your life.

Three

ON THE ALTAR OF SACRIFICE

WHEN I ARRIVED home, I started to read the story of Abraham's life. I focused on it for the next four months. Every time I opened my Bible and read carefully about Abraham, the father of faith, the Holy Spirit spoke to me. In these next chapters I will point out some of the things God showed me. This was not the beginning of the process of renewal in my life; God had already started it. However, it was here that I became aware that He was renewing me. Be ready. God will also speak to you.

Generally, when we read about Abraham we start at Genesis 12. This time, however, let's start at chapter 11:

> This is the account of Terah. Terah became the father of Abram, Nahor and Haran. And Haran became the father of Lot.
>
> —GENESIS 11:27

Abram's father was Terah. "Terah took his son Abram, his grandson Lot son of Haran, and his daughter-in-law Sarai, the wife of his son Abram, and together they set out from Ur of the Chaldeans to go to Canaan. But when they came to Haran, they settled there" (v. 31).

This passage really surprised me. God had only called Abram. His mandate to him had been clear: "Leave your country, your people and your father's household and go to the land I will show you" (Gen. 12:1).

Hispanics know that fathers are honored. Our fathers are the heads of the family. They have the right to give us direction, advice, and to point us in the right direction. I'm sure that Abram felt the same. Terah was his father. He was the head of the clan. He was also their priest. In those days, the father was the priest; he represented the family before the gods. When Abram announced that God had told him to leave his native land, Terah took on the leadership. If Abram, his son, was going to leave, Terah had to be the leader of the expedition to Canaan. As such, he took Abram, Sarai, and Lot, his dear grandson.

God had given Abram a general direction. The Promised Land was in Canaan. That's where Terah, Abram, Sarai, and Lot headed. When they arrived at the city of Haran, they stopped. I'm sure Terah decided to stay there. At that point, Terah, who was directing Abram, became a hindrance to him.

Joshua told the Israelites in Joshua 24:2: "This is what the LORD, the God of Israel, says: 'Long ago your forefathers, including Terah the father of Abraham and Nahor, lived beyond the River and worshiped other gods.'"

Haran was a commercial and religious center situated along a road frequently traveled by armies and caravans of merchants. The archeological excavations performed in this region revealed that the city had a temple dedicated to Sin, the moon god. The name *Haran* means "a dry and arid place, a place that has been burnt." Abram lived in this idolatrous, dry city by order of his father, Terah.

Terah represented a cultural, religious, and mental bondage to Abram. Terah served foreign gods. Like every head of a family clan, Terah was the priest of the god Sin. God's mandate to leave the homeland was to Abram only (Isa. 51:2). But it was only after Terah's death that Abram was free to leave Haran and go to the land God was to show him (Gen. 11:32; 12:4). When he departed, Abram was able to leave behind his family's idolatrous influences. Then God started to reveal Himself more clearly to Abram. The first transformation in Abram's life came as the result of his father's death.

> I will make you into a great nation
>   and I will bless you;
> I will make your name great,
>   and you will be a blessing.
> I will bless those who bless you,
>   and whoever curses you I will curse;
> and all peoples on earth
>   will be blessed through you.
>
> —GENESIS 12:2–3

God would show Abram the land, but God was going to have to perform a miracle in order to produce descendants—Sarai was barren.

However, there is a huge distance between a prophecy and its fulfillment. Abram received the initial promise in which God was showing him the land. However, he stopped on the way because he was tied to his father and his culture. When he cut himself off from his father, his culture, and his family beliefs, he began to receive clear direction from God.

One day, he "set out for the land of Canaan" and arrived at "the site of the great tree of Moreh at Shechem" (Gen. 12:5–6). There he encountered a problem. Canaan, the territory promised by God, was occupied by the Canaanites. In that moment of doubt, "the LORD appeared to Abram and said, 'To your offspring I will give this land.' So he built an altar there to the LORD, who had appeared to him" (Gen. 12:7).

God promised him "the land." Abram had already set his foot on the land even though he had not conquered it yet. While in Ur, God could not promise him "the land." In

Haran, God didn't tell him where the Promised Land was. However, when he left his clan, his security, and arrived at an unknown and uncertain place occupied by hostile people, God showed him a little bit more of the vision. What did Abram do? He worshiped. He built an altar (12:7). Then he went toward Bethel, pitched his tent, built another altar, and "called on the name of the LORD" (12:8). For the first time, a man publicly and openly invokes the name of his God in front of those who were dwelling in the land of Canaan.

God spoke very directly to me as I studied Abram's response to God's call. I could no longer lean on my partners, leaders, family, and friends. How difficult it is to obey God when He commands us to lean only on Him. We prefer to talk about our needs with our brothers and sisters, looking for their compassion. We ask everybody to pray. We call out to God, complaining about the pain. But I had to trust God, even when there were threats. I had to overlook the circumstances and build altars of worship to the Lord.

In the following months, my prayer was: "Lord, I don't know how to worship You; help me! Lord, I don't know how to trust in You; teach me! I want to worship and bow down before this altar, but I don't know how to do that. Teach me!"

WITH A "LOT" IN THE HEART

ABRAM WAS ON his way to being transformed and renewed. Me, too. However, there was still much to do. Lot, Abram's nephew, was still with him. Even though I didn't have a person who represented the concept of "Lot" in my life, I had a *Lot* in my heart.

In Genesis 13, Abram and Lot stayed together. Abram had a different lifestyle than Lot. Although they were both wealthy, only Abram invoked the name of Jehovah and built altars. Lot's focus was centered on his many sheep, cows, and tents. Success and prosperity without God bring conflicts. Soon the quarreling began between the servants of Abram and Lot. Abram and Lot reached an agreement: They had to part company and go different ways.

Abram let Lot choose a portion of the land first. In Genesis 13:10, we can observe Lot's behavior: "Lot looked up."

That was the beginning. Lot examined the territory. He was an expert and had knowledge of the territory. There is nothing wrong with looking up; it all depends where we direct our eyes.

> Lot...saw that the whole plain of the Jordan was well watered, like the garden of the LORD, like the land of Egypt, toward Zoar. (This was before the LORD destroyed Sodom and Gomorrah.)
>
> —GENESIS 13:10

After looking, Lot analyzed the situation carefully. When he saw the valley of the Jordan toward Sodom and Gomorrah, he got excited. He thought the territory looked like the garden of the Lord.

Apparently, what he saw was so beautiful it looked like the concept he had of the Garden of Eden. However, a very well-known proverb says, "All that glitters is not gold." That proverb reflects a very powerful spiritual truth. Not everything that presents itself as promising, positive, comfortable, practical, and well recommended is from God.

Lot chose the whole plain of the Jordan for himself. He chose what looked good. When one hasn't completely surrendered his life to the Lord, he analyzes things from a practical point of view. If something works, then it is good; if everybody is in agreement, if it brings happiness and success, it must be from God. We frequently make decisions by looking at circumstances, people, and appearances. We decide to do what seems practical.

That is how Lot chose. Lot went toward the east. He set out in the opposite direction of the blessing of God. Lot was leaving the blessing behind. The blessing was in Abram, not in the land. Lot had parted from a blessed and anointed man.

Abram's decision was different. The following verses reveal his choice: "The LORD said to Abram after Lot had parted from him, 'Lift up your eyes'" (Gen. 13:14). Lot had lifted up his eyes without waiting on God. He looked in the direction that seemed good. Abram was an altar builder, a worshiper. He knew how to wait on God. When God gave him the order, he lifted up his eyes.

"From where you are...look north and south, east and west" (v. 14). Where was Abram? In the place of worship, by the altar, between Bethel and Ai. *Bethel* means "house of God," and *Ai* means "ruins." Abram was worshiping God between the ruins and the glory of God. What a tremendous place. What a tremendous lesson. From that place, Abram could see the land with a clear, well-informed mind. From the place of worship, God's plans and purposes can be seen so clearly. Abram could discern that he was in the place of decision.

Lot could only see what looked beautiful but in reality was destructive. Abram, from the place of worship, saw the blessing. In the place of worship, God tells him that his descendants will be too numerous to count. In the place of worship, God tells Abram to get up and walk the length and the breadth of the land that already belonged to him. From the place of worship, Abram stepped onto the land that God had promised him.

Abram then moved his tents and went to live near the great trees of Mamre at Hebron; there he built an altar to the Lord. How did Abram end up near the great trees of Mamre? God led him there. One day, the Lord and His two angels would come to Mamre and visit Abram and Sarai to announce the birth of their son, Isaac, and the destruction of Sodom and Gomorrah (Gen. 18). In the place of worship, God doesn't "hide" His will from us; He treats us like friends.

How did Lot's life end? Sitting at Sodom's gateway (Gen. 19:1). Only the leaders of the city sat at the main gate. Lot ended up being a leader in Sodom, calling the Sodomites "friends" and offering his own daughters to the Sodomites to do what they chose with them. (See Genesis 19:7–8.) Finally, Lot lost his wife. He ended up destroyed, drunk in a cave, and committing incest with his two daughters. From this horrible union came his descendants: Moab, the father of the Moabites, and Ben-Ammi, the father of the Ammonites. Both were enemies of God and of His people, Israel.

How did Abraham's life end? Read Jesus' genealogy in the first chapter of the Gospel of Matthew. Abraham was the father of Isaac, Isaac the father of Jacob, Jacob the father of the tribes of Israel, from which comes King David, and from him come Mary and Joseph, the parents of our Lord Jesus, the Messiah, the blessing of all the families on the earth.

Abram was on the right path. In the fifteenth chapter of Genesis, God appears to him in a vision and repeats the promise of an offspring: "Do not be afraid, Abram. I am your shield, your very great reward" (v. 1).

What encouraging words! What comforting words! Abram was on the right path.

HEADING FOR RENEWAL

ABRAM HADN'T REACHED the place of the miracle yet. In verse 2, we read: "But Abram said, 'O Sovereign LORD, what can you give me since I remain childless?'" He was still thinking about the promise, the blessing, the way God would provide.

This is exactly what I was going through on my way toward renewal. Several questions were tormenting me: *What is God going to do to free me from these false accusations of fraud in the ministry? How will He do it? How long will it take?* I trusted in God, but the situation was getting

34

worse. More meetings were taking place. More people were speaking against me from another radio station. I was accused of belonging to the Mafia, hiring some hit men to threaten a family, and destroying a car. Somebody came to our radio station and asked malicious questions while recording everything on tape. Others initiated police investigations into my personal affairs. My name was being tarnished.

During those months, God told me not to do anything. I was not to defend myself or talk about the issue. I couldn't make any comments when others informed me what my critics were saying. God was ordering me to be still.

Now we arrive at the true message from Abram's experience. The Bible says:

> When Abram was ninety-nine years old, the LORD appeared to him and said, "I am God Almighty; walk before me and be blameless."
>
> —GENESIS 17:1

Abram was ninety-nine years old. He was an elderly man, no longer able to father children. At his worst moment, when nothing else could be done, God Almighty appeared to him. For the very first time in the Bible, God revealed Himself using the name *El Shaddai*. This name comes from the word *shad,* which means "breast." The name *El Shaddai* describes a picture of a mother nursing her child until the baby is completely satisfied. El Shaddai is the God who is more than sufficient, He who satisfies us completely.

Nothing satisfies children more than their mother's milk. Not only is their thirst satisfied, but the children also receive the mother's warmth by being in her arms several times a day, including very late at night. My children spent four or five hours per day in the tender arms of their mother, very close to her heartbeat. From there they simply looked up at their mother's smile and listened to her voice; they felt secure and loved. This is the concept expressed by the

35

name *El Shaddai*. God holds us in His arms. He comforts us, patiently assists us, feeds us until we are satisfied, talks tenderly to us, and makes us feel totally secure.

El Shaddai appeared in the life of Abraham to "greatly increase his numbers" (Gen. 17:2). But He didn't reveal Himself to Abram until Abram could no longer produce anything. When Abram died to self, El Shaddai revealed Himself.

El Shaddai appears in deserts, in trials, and in difficult times. The widow Naomi says in Ruth 1:20, "Don't call me Naomi.... Call me Mara, because the Almighty [*El Shaddai*] has made my life very bitter."

El Shaddai is mentioned thirty-one times in the Book of Job, the prototype of the believer who goes through a trial. El Shaddai is the God who reveals Himself when there is no way out, when there is no solution available. El Shaddai is the God who comes to the desert to multiply, to bring forth fruit, to renew. But when does He come? When we die to our skills, our strength, and our abilities. El Shaddai manifested Himself in Job's life when he stopped justifying himself, when he stopped asking why all the calamities hit his life, and when he stopped questioning God. When Job surrendered and recognized that neither he nor his friends could understand the things of God, El Shaddai spoke, comforted, and gave him back everything he had lost, giving him twice as much as he had before (Job 42:10).

Job had not spoken what was right about God, but he repented. His friends didn't repent—they were wise and full of their own knowledge. When God's wrath burned against them, they went to Job to ask him to pray for them.

Like Job, Abram bowed down and worshiped El Shaddai. He couldn't reason or argue with God. He was too old. He had already tried unsuccessfully. When he tried to produce offspring by his own devices, he produced Ishmael, a problem child, fruit of the works of the flesh. Now he was exhausted. When Abram surrendered, El Shaddai revealed Himself.

In that moment of worship, bowing down before the majestic authority of El Shaddai, Abram put himself in the hands of the Almighty. And God acted. In Genesis 17:5, God says, "No longer will you be called Abram; your name will be Abraham, for I have made you a father of many nations."

A COVENANT IS AN EXCHANGE OF LIVES

IN THE PLACE of worship, God made a covenant with Abram. When two people made a biblical covenant, they promised to be a friend to their friend's friends and an enemy to their friend's enemies; they shared debts as well as riches. They swore friendship and loyalty, and they sealed it with the shedding of the blood of animals. El Shaddai made a covenant with Abram. Abram gave God his old body, incapable of producing an heir, nearly dead; God gave Abram multiplied generations of nations and kings. Abram gave God death; God gave Abram life. Abram, the exalted father, gave God his name; El Shaddai gave him another name in return—*Abraham,* father of many nations.

In that place of total surrender God changes and renews us. God renewed Abram, who became Abraham.

That very same day, God changed Abram's name—and His own. From that day on, God made Himself known as the "God of Abraham." God sealed the covenant with Abraham and gave His name as the signature. This same God dealt with me in the midst of my chaotic situation.

When El Shaddai appears, He always asks for something. He asked Abraham to walk before Him and be blameless. How can anyone walk before God and be blameless? There is only one way—by dying to self. We must die to what we see with our eyes, to our talents and skills, and to our own opinions, reasonings, and solutions. We depend totally on God and wait on Him. There is only one way of walking before God: being in His presence. Do what Job did, who recognized that all he could do was ask, listen, and learn from God.

How did Abraham come out of that situation? Can we say that everything was instantly fixed? No! Abraham still had problems.

His age was a problem—he was ninety-nine years old. The writer of the Book of Hebrews says that Abraham was "as good as dead" (Heb. 11:12).

Another problem was that Abraham still lived in a tent—he didn't live in a city. A tent is not a permanent place to live. In those days, nomads lived in tents, traveling from one place to another, never settling permanently in any place. Abraham lived like a nomad, "like a stranger in a foreign country" (Heb. 11:9). He didn't have any rights, privileges, or citizenship. The Canaanites treated Abraham like an immigrant and an outsider, possibly even like an invader. That land was a "foreign" land to him.

Abraham was "looking forward" to the city with foundations (v. 10). A tent has no foundations; it is temporarily pitched on a piece of land. With a tent, if one has to move, he can quickly pack, take the tent down, and go somewhere else. Abraham didn't go. Abraham learned that God was going to build the promised city. He had to stay in his tent. He had to wait on the architect and constructor—God, El Shaddai.

In my own desperate situation, while the situation was getting worse and the accusations were increasing, God showed me that I had to "die." I had to surrender to His hands. I had to remain silent before the accusations and wait for El Shaddai to perform a miracle. I had to stay in that unstable, dangerous situation without putting together a defense. God would build this house. I had to remain in the tent of faith, willing to be treated like a stranger, an accused man in a foreign land. I had to forgive those who were hurting me, and I had to pray for them. I had to behave like a stranger who didn't have the right to receive justice. It was difficult because I didn't know God's ways very well. I didn't know Him in this aspect, but I learned to know Him in the desert, in weakness, and in pain.

God teaches us that in order for Him to use our lives, we have to go through a process of brokenness. In the process of renewal, God shows us our pride, our self-sufficiency, and our sinfulness through trials. If you want to be close to God and want to have God close to you, allow Him to break you.

> The LORD is close to the brokenhearted and saves those who are crushed in spirit.
>
> —PSALM 34:18

I thought I could achieve whatever I set out to do. My parents instilled in me a very healthy self-esteem. But God doesn't accept this. In renewal, the Holy Spirit will bring our hidden carnality to light and will break us so we can become broken vessels in the hands of God. My first confession was simple: I can't please God in my own strength. My life as a model Christian is not enough. My ministerial achievements aren't enough.

The Holy Spirit will never be able to renew our lives if we are not broken by our absolute inability to please God. He will never transform us if we don't admit our total need to be cleansed, purified, and washed from our sins. God was preparing me for an encounter. He was about to make a covenant with me. But before the covenant, before the renewal, before the manifestation of His glory, it is necessary to die on the altar of brokenness.

If you are going through an impossible situation, God is ready to make a covenant with you. The first step is to abandon all plans, all designs, all hope in your knowledge, friends, family, and resources. He who abandons himself in the arms of El Shaddai will be totally satisfied. He will be the architect of your way out. In the meantime, you stay and wait for Him to begin the construction.

Abraham never saw that promised city; neither did his son Isaac, his grandson Jacob, or even Joseph, his great-grandson. However, Joseph had so much faith that he ordered his bones to be buried in the Promised Land. God's works take time, but they transcend from generation to generation. Trust in God. Even though you don't see the fulfillment of the promises in your own lifetime, don't be afraid! He can fulfill them in the lifetime of your sons and your grandsons.

Four hundred years later, God raised up Moses to lead Abraham's people, the people of the promise, out of Egypt. Even though Moses didn't go into the Promised Land, Joshua did. Joshua established cities—no more temporary tents, but houses with foundations. After some time, the kingdom of Israel was established. This happened hundreds of years after Abraham. He believed it was going to happen when he died to his self, to his flesh, and to his ability to achieve the promise with his own strength. When did he surrender? He did it when he was ninety-nine years old.

I hope you won't take that long to surrender. Surrender to the Lord. Allow Him to be your defender, your lawyer, and your head of public relations. *El Shaddai,* "He who is more than sufficient," is your God!

Four

_____

SELAH

THE FOLLOWING MONTHS were very difficult. On the one hand, God was teaching me to die on the altar of sacrifice. The sacrifice was not money, a career, or a dream. The sacrifice was myself. Even though this wasn't a pleasant process, I was certain God was working. On the other hand, the situation wasn't changing.

During those days, God surrounded me with His presence in a way I had never known. I had known God as my Lord, my boss, my King, my director, and my leader. I was only now beginning to know Him as *El Shaddai,* my refuge, my father, my mother, my friend, my brother, my pastor, my doctor, my nurse, my provider, my all. In those months, I decided not to listen to the negative reports. I told my coworkers not to tell me the rumors. I closed my ears to all the calumnies.

For four months, I focused all my attention on what God was doing in me. When one surrenders into the hands of the Almighty, one doesn't defend oneself, doesn't act, and doesn't explain. One simply waits for God, the attorney, to execute. I was waiting for Him to miraculously quiet my accusers, shame them publicly, and to directly intervene. However, that didn't happen. He is the One who works.

And when He does, He does it incredibly well. He doesn't use our mechanisms. He is an innovator! I have to confess that I was surprised.

A PROVIDENTIAL INVITATION

ONE AFTERNOON, SOME dear friends from Argentina came to visit me on their way to another city. They were going to attend a miracle crusade led by Pastor Benny Hinn, the preacher God used to speak to me four months earlier. The brothers from Argentina were excited. They had come all the way from Argentina to be touched by God. My friend Omar Daldi had brought one of the most important leaders of the church in Argentina, Pastor Pedro Ibarra. When I met with Pastor Ibarra, I realized that I was sitting before a very humble person, someone who had placed himself completely in God's hands.

Pedro Ibarra told me what God was doing in his country, particularly in his church. He described glorious things to me. Even though I rejoiced with Pastor Ibarra, I thought that what he was telling me was meant for Argentina only. God was revolutionizing the church in that country. He told me how they had to remove the people who were "drunk" from the services, those who had been powerfully touched by God. God's presence, the "anointing" of the Holy Spirit, was so irresistible that hundreds of people were collapsing, then rising healed, set free, comforted, and filled with the Holy Spirit.

They invited me to go with them to a crusade in Toronto, Canada. Although my brother Ruben had already made plans to go, I decided not to go. I was busy and totally focused on what God was doing in my life.

At three o'clock that afternoon, as the brothers were saying good-bye, I felt that God was pushing me to go with them to the crusade. I obeyed immediately, called the travel agency, and miraculously was able to get tickets.

I had never attended one of Pastor Benny Hinn's crusades.

Even though I had been to his church in Orlando and had seen many of his crusades on video, I wasn't prepared to witness what I was to see. As I came into the big hockey stadium, I felt as if I had entered a powerhouse. More than twenty thousand people were worshiping Jesus and welcoming the Holy Spirit. That night, God performed incredible miracles of healing. Even though I was used to seeing miracles, I wasn't used to Pastor Benny's style. He didn't pray for any of the sick in particular. He simply worshiped by singing, praying, and leading the crowd to honor the presence of Jesus the Healer. At a certain point in the middle of worship, he started to declare that the sick were being touched and healed by Jesus. Suddenly, there were shouts of joy; people started to run up front to testify. It was a wonderful service.

The next evening, we were able to sit in the front row of the auditorium, right in front of the platform. I felt incredibly hungry. I wanted to be God's instrument—but in a different way than Pastor Benny Hinn. God used him for healing and miracles in the anointing. I didn't believe I had that same calling. God had called me to work in radio ministry, to teach, to invade new territories with international television and radio. I wasn't an evangelist. When the time came to pray for the sick, I always looked for somebody else to do it. There, in the first row of that service, I was waiting for God to touch me, to strengthen me, and to anoint me to continue working on the task that had been entrusted to me.

"WHAT ARE YOU DOING, HOLY SPIRIT?"

AT A GIVEN moment during the worship, Pastor Benny stopped the music. He announced that for two weeks he had been feeling a special burden for some of the people God wanted to touch that night. He immediately came down from the platform and headed toward the people sitting in the first row. When he laid his hands on my head, I felt the power of the Holy Spirit penetrate my body from head to toe. I fell flat on my face. Imagine—I used to laugh at those who fell; now it was happening to me. I don't know how long I stayed there. I didn't faint; I knew what was happening, but the Holy Spirit was working in me. In those moments, God filled me with His presence. I had never felt it in such a glorious way. Finally they lifted me up. When I went back to my seat, I thanked the Holy Spirit for the glorious "experience" I had just had. That night, I knew that God had manifested His presence and His glory over me just as He had done with Moses, Isaiah, Paul, and many others.

I returned to the radio station to reassume my responsibilities, one of them being to participate in the end-of-the-year radio marathon. During those weeks, we suspended all our regular programming to collect funds to defray the radio ministry's expenses. We needed a million dollars to cover our budget.

That afternoon I was supposed to go on the air to preach and make an appeal to the supporters. On my way to the studio, I sensed something different. A longing to worship the Lord through the vehicle of our live radio broadcasts was born within me. This had never been done. Rapidly I looked for worship music, but I was unable to find much variety.

Our radio station preferred to play popular Christian music interpreted by well-known Christian artists. We could find only two or three worship music recordings. Yet I wanted to worship the Lord. In the Toronto crusade I had seen and experienced the powerful move of the Holy Spirit in the midst of the worship. No one had shouted, no one had raised his voice, but in the sweet, slow, and deep adoration and exaltation of our Lord Jesus Christ, God had touched thousands—and had revolutionized my heart. I wanted to do the same on the radio. I wanted to worship Christ, knowing it would please the Holy Spirit. Only a few hours earlier, I had seen that the Holy Spirit delights in worship. He starts to spread virtue, grace, health, blessing, mercy, and power when we welcome Him.

We went on the air to *worship*. Generally, during the radio marathons, our focus was to preach or ask for offerings. Now, however, I was going on the air to worship live, and I had very little inclination to ask for an offering. The worship music started to flow through the atmosphere. I left the microphone on, something you don't do on radio. But this time, as I heard the music in my headphones, I started to sing. Suddenly I started to cry. The radio engineer continued to play music, and I kept on praying, crying, worshiping, and praising the Lord with the microphone on. I had done this in the privacy of my home before, but now I was doing it publicly.

Under the glorious manifestation of His presence in that studio, I confessed my sins, failures, and weaknesses. I didn't realize thousands were listening to me. I was simply aware that I was prostrating myself before the majestic throne of Jesus Christ, our King. Without realizing it, I worshiped the Lord live for more than two hours. I forgot I was in a studio. I forgot about the marathon, the radio formats, the audience, the people around me, everything. I was worshiping from my heart, in spirit and in truth.

When I opened my eyes, the announcer and staff answering the phones informed me that hundreds of people were calling—the presence of God was manifesting in their homes and they couldn't remain standing. Some had received miraculous healings, others had been filled with the Holy Spirit, several had called to receive Jesus Christ as their personal Savior, and many others were delivered instantly from demonic oppressions.

I was the one who was most surprised. This had never happened before. Such things happened only when some dynamic evangelist came to the radio station. For me it was something new. We decided to put some of the phone calls on the air. During the next three hours, we received call after call declaring the great wonders that take place when the Holy Spirit manifests His presence with power.

WORSHIP INSTEAD OF MARATHON

THE NEXT DAY, once again we worshiped God with worship music and praise. We left the microphones on and allowed the Holy Spirit to work without any time limitations. The same thing happened again. Calls testifying to miracles, healing, salvation, and deliverance started to rain on us.

During that month of the marathon, we didn't ask for any money; we didn't present any financial need. Yet all the money we needed came through the mail. As they witnessed the great manifestation of the Holy Spirit through the radio, the people of God sent the necessary amount of money to cover our annual budget. God performed a miracle. When did He do it? The moment we stopped trying to convince the people to send offerings. When we worship God, we direct our eyes and our heart to Him, and we lead others to do the same. There El Shaddai manifests Himself and multiplies.

This caused a great impact in the city. The people were asking what was going on, why we had changed the music, why we were playing worship and praise music, scriptural music. The presence of the Holy Spirit was manifesting in a tangible way every time we started to worship Him and sing songs of praise. In those moments of adoration, the Holy Spirit started to teach us to worship in spirit and in truth. I learned to be transparent with God and with the listeners; the masks, the ministry professionalism, went up in smoke. My usual way of praying, worshiping, and praising became a sweet dialogue with Christ.

After some weeks, we found out that this radio worship phenomenon wasn't happening just in New York. It was a move of God all over Latin America. We were joining this new move of God late; God had been renewing the worship and praise of the church for several years.

What happened to the criticisms? When God manifested

Himself on the radio in such a public way, those who were planning my destruction were silenced. Those who were listening to my accusers realized that God had poured a new anointing over the radio station and over those who worked there. In the face of all that evidence of public fruits, the mouths were closed shut.

That is how I came to experience the God who is "my glory, and the lifter of my head" (Ps. 3:3, KJV). When He lifts our heads, He does it by pouring out His glory over us. How many times do we try to impress people with our knowledge? How many times do we try to project ourselves, making ourselves known by talking to others about our experiences, our studies, and our circle of friends? How useless all that is! How ignorant we are! How glorious it is when we don't speak, when we don't project ourselves, demanding honor, respect, or position! It is beautiful when God pours out His glory on our lives; those who are watching us can see what He produces in us. I desired this many times. Now it was happening.

This period in my life was glorious, even though it was simply the first touch—a new revelation of God in my life. Some told me that I should organize mass meetings. Others were already planning things for me to do.

I stopped; I didn't know what to do. I immediately asked God for direction. At that moment, the ministry wasn't the most important thing for me. I was only interested in knowing God and learning to practice His presence. The more I worshiped, the more God showed me the changes that He had to perform in my heart. The more I sought Him, the more I could see my needs, my weaknesses, and my sins.

One afternoon at home, before leaving to attend a ministry commitment, God instructed me to go to the office. As I entered my office, I automatically grabbed a chair at which to kneel. Instead I felt urged to open the Bible. Even though I always read a certain Bible, I found another Bible on my desk. I opened it, and my eyes focused on Psalm 3, specifically on the word *selah*. I knew *selah* means "pause" in a musical sense. Suddenly I felt a strong desire to immerse myself in this psalm. I knew it very well; I had read it a great many times, and we had sung it in our church. However, it was different this time. God was trying to show me something.

A HUGE CALAMITY

LET ME SHARE with you what God showed me through Psalm 3, one of the first steps toward renewal.

King David wrote Psalm 3. At the time of the writing of this psalm, no longer is he the young shepherd running away from King Saul's jealousy. He is now the king of Israel. He has conquered all his enemies and is at the height of his success.

Yet, here we see him in the midst of much distress. Absalom, his own beloved son, is pursuing him to kill him. His own son wants to take the throne away from him. His own son is destroying his character, his testimony, and his life. Even though David, a victorious warrior, is used to fighting face to face with his enemies, he will not do it this time. The enemy is his son, blood of his blood and bone of his bones. So he runs away to the desert; there he writes another psalm, Psalm 63. From that arid place, this man who had been very courageous says these words:

> O God, you are my God, earnestly I seek you; my soul thirsts for you, my body longs for you, in a dry and weary land where there is no water.
>
> —PSALM 63:1

David was in a desert without any water; he was in a dry and weary land, alone and persecuted by his enemies. His desire was to seek God, to behold His power and His glory in the way he had contemplated it so many times in the sanctuary (v. 2).

In Psalm 3, however, he begins to complain. His situation is not an invention; he isn't dreaming. The first thing he does is to take a look at how things are. "How many are my foes!" (v. 1). Absalom wasn't alone; he had organized a powerful conspiracy against his father the king. Even some of David's old friends were teaming up with David's rebellious son. They were not only speaking against David; they were armed and planning to kill him. David did not say in vain, "Many are saying of me, 'God will not deliver him'" (v. 2).

Those who hated him were hoping to kill him. His friends didn't give him any hope. Those who knew him understood that the situation had not presented itself by sheer chance—it was God's judgment. David had sinned many years ago. He had taken a woman that didn't belong to him. Her name was Bathsheba, daughter of Eliam and granddaughter of Ahithophel, an old friend of David's and now Absalom's main counselor.

The past had finally caught up with David. Nathan had prophesied to him that God's judgment was going to be manifested in his house and that he was going to be publicly shamed. Ahithophel wanted vengeance. Absalom wanted to be king. God had promised judgment because of Uriah's hidden murder and David's shameless adultery with Bathsheba. David was surrounded. There was no escape.

As I sat there in my office reading my Bible, I wondered why God had led me to go to my office; I could have prayed at home. But God is very wise. The Bible I was reading (an old one that I have on my desk) had the word *selah* printed in bold. The Holy Spirit stopped me abruptly at that word.

Then I continued to read. In verse 3, David is transformed. Out of a desperate heart, stuck in the desert with no way out, he says these words: "But you are a shield around me, O LORD; you bestow glory on me and lift up my head."

Something happened to David—and it changed him. In spite of his enemies, he suddenly confessed that God was his shield, his glory, and his defense lawyer. What had happened?

I believe David took a *selah,* a musical pause. He took his harp and sang melodies to the Lord right in the midst of the dry and arid desert. When he took a *selah,* he came back to his senses. From his better perspective, he could say, "God is a 'shield around me!'"

If something or someone raises up against me, before he can touch me, he has to go through the shield around me. If something or someone wants to hurt or destroy me, he has to go through my Lord. He is a shield. God covers me from the enemies whom I see coming and from those who attack me from behind. God is my shield!

David continues by saying that Jehovah is his glory. The word *glory* has several meanings. In this case, it expresses "excellence, praise, honor, the best." For David, the lofty thing in that moment was not his palace, his crown, his reputation, his influence, or his power. His glory, the excellent thing, was God Himself—plainly and simply God. The fact that he could sing to Him, call Him by His name, and know that He was listening to him was enough.

Knowing that He is my God is the most sublime, the most important thing in my life. And the blessings…the rewards…the results? Although we need His blessings, we *have to have* an intimate relationship with God, not because of the benefits He provides, but because He is our Creator, our Father, our life, the meaning of it all, the Most High.

David declared that God was the lifter of his head. All his enemies were putting him to shame. There was no defense for him. He had decided to stop defending himself from all the lies. (See Psalm 39.) God was his only defense, the only One who could maintain the reputation and the name of David on high.

God was speaking to me. Like David, I needed to rest, to take a *selah*. In the middle of the desert of accusations and uncertainty, I had to sing, worship, and do what David did in Psalm 3:5–7:

I lie down and sleep; I wake again, because the LORD

sustains me. I will not fear the tens of thousands drawn up against me on every side. Arise, O LORD! Deliver me, O my God!

God told me, "Rest! Sleep in peace. Don't let threats frighten you! Sing! Delight yourself in the worship songs! When you feel burdened, close the door and start to sing, to rest, to lean on Me." God was sustaining me, waking me up if there was danger and giving me restful sleep. The psalm concludes with these words: "From the LORD comes deliverance. May your blessing be on your people" (v. 8).

ALWAYS WITH US

THE SOLUTION BELONGS to our Lord. Salvation is not in our hands, but in God's. The blessing, the manifestation of salvation, is over us. It doesn't come and go or reappear every once in a while—it is continually resting over us. No matter what circumstances we may be going through, God's blessing surrounds us; it is our shield and our glory.

The secret of effective prayer is to rest, to wait, to *selah*. As long as we make an effort to solve our problems or worry about the way in which God is going to work or how long He will take to do it, we will be weak and defeated Christians. We will not see renewal in our spiritual lives.

I was concerned about God's will in my life. What would this new experience require? Would I have to change my way of ministering? Would I have to hold rallies? Would I have to pray for the sick? Would I have to pray and fast until I found an answer? Would my life change?

That afternoon in my office, God showed me a way—the way of worship, of rest, of waiting on Him. The Lord sent me to rest and to wait on Him.

Since that day, I close my door and put on worship music—melodies declaring His greatness, declaring the Word of God in music and in rest. As I hear the Word of God in a song, faith comes. When I worship, I direct my attention to

Him—to His name, to the Savior of my life, to my shield, to the lifter of my head, to the One who loves me.

And the accusations? My future? People's opinions? What if someone takes us to court with false accusations? Who would defend us? How much money would we spend in lawyers' fees and in legal defense? What would our supporters, the listeners, say? What would the press say? All these questions and dilemmas vanish in the mind of the person who rests in the Lord and sings:

> Then sings my soul, my Saviour God, to Thee:
> How great Thou art! How great Thou art!
> Then sings my soul, my Saviour God, to Thee:
> How great Thou art! How great Thou art!*

Our minds can't handle two thoughts at the same time. He who rests in the Lord—who takes a *selah,* who focuses his mind on God, who sleeps, knowing that God sustains him—will demolish all arguments and every pretension that sets itself up against the knowledge of God in his life.

Those who witnessed the change performed by the Holy Spirit in me noticed the fruits, the anointing, and the results in the lives of the listeners to whom we ministered.

I saw something else; I saw the inner changes that God was making. First, I learned to worship Him in spirit and in truth. Then, I learned to pray (to have communion with Him). I also learned how easy it was to search the Scriptures once worship and communion with Him had softened my heart. As I received insights from the Word of God, the Spirit instructed me on how to minister to others by preaching and by prophetic words of edification and exhortation. The people responded, and the Holy Spirit taught me to minister to them individually. God was taking me to a new place. He was renewing me.

---

*"How Great Thou Art," copyright © 1953, S. K. Hine. Assigned to Manna Music, Inc., 35255 Brooten Road, Pacific City, OR 97135. Renewed 1981. All rights reserved. Used by permission. (ASCAP)

Five

IN THE DESERT OF THE SPIRIT

DURING THE FIRST months of my renewal, I saw many wonderful manifestations of God's power in my life and in the lives of others. I had to change my radio program frequently because the Holy Spirit manifested His power in the lives of the listeners, and therefore we couldn't go off the air. The normal duration was about two hours, but sometimes it extended to four, five, and even eight hours. On more than one occasion I didn't want to leave the studio because God's presence was so real.

You will probably think: *How wonderful!* It's true, and I was the most surprised of all at what God was doing.

Some of the people who worked with me encouraged me to organize evangelistic crusades, services of deliverance and healing, but I understood that I shouldn't do that. God was still working in me, and He wasn't done yet. I, for my part, wanted to be sure that the change wasn't temporary. I wanted to be sure this new anointing would remain, that in six months I wasn't going to be the person I used to be. Therefore, I waited. God kept changing me. I was entering a period of transformation.

My first encounter with God was powerful. I fell down and cried like a baby; I shuddered. In other words, there was a real revolution taking place in me. However, that was only the first touch, God's initial step. And then? No man can seek God unless God is seeking him first. In that first encounter, God sought me, and He found me. What would come next? Would this experience be enough for me? I decided to seek more.

Jesus is our example. We say this many times, but we don't practice it. The writer of the Book of Hebrews exhorts us to set our eyes on Christ Jesus, to hold Him constantly as our model. That is what I needed—to know Jesus as my model.

WAIT, IT'S WORTH IT

IN THAT GLORIOUS meeting in Toronto, the Holy Spirit filled me with His presence. His presence transforms and affects. I had never experienced the manifestation of the Spirit like that. I wondered, *What would come next? What would Jesus have done?*

I decided to wait for the Holy Spirit to conform me to the image of Christ. I wanted to do what Christ would have done if He had been in my place. In the following months I would learn to walk in God's ways.

Before starting His ministry, Jesus went from Galilee to the Jordan so that John could baptize Him. John the Baptist was a controversial preacher. He preached repentance. The people who listened to him would confess their sins, and as a sign of repentance, John would baptize them. To be put under the waters by John the Baptist was a public sign of confession of guilt and of purification of sins.

John was surprised when he saw Jesus, the Lamb of God who takes away sin, coming to him to be baptized, and so he objected. He said that instead of baptizing Jesus, he needed Jesus to baptize him. In Matthew 3:15, Jesus said, "Let it be so now; it is proper for us to do this to fulfill all righteousness."

John may have needed to see the sign of the Holy Spirit on Jesus, but Jesus also needed the fullness of the Holy

Spirit. Without that fullness, Jesus—the second Adam—our representative, could not start His ministry. Jesus, our example, needed to be filled with the power of the Holy Spirit; without it, He could not accomplish His mission. By allowing John to baptize Him, Jesus humbled Himself. The most important thing for Him was the manifestation of the Spirit, His fullness, and the investiture that the third person of the Trinity would give Him.

At the precise moment when Jesus rose out of the water, the heavens were opened. The Holy Spirit descended like a dove and alighted on Him. The Holy Spirit came; He made His appearance, and for the very first time He filled a man—Jesus the man. Until that moment, the Spirit would descend on men and women, use them, and then leave. This time He descended on Jesus of Nazareth and didn't leave, but He stayed to fill Him and to invest Him with power for the execution of the will of the Father in the power of the Spirit. The Spirit touched Him, filled Him, and anointed Him.

The Father spoke from heaven: "This is my Son, whom I love; with him I am well pleased" (Matt. 3:17).

What a glorious experience! The Holy Spirit had arrived. Jesus could now start His ministry. He, however, had not yet completed His preparation. Even though the Holy Spirit had anointed Him and the Father had declared His absolute pleasure, Jesus now had to go into the desert.

THE DESERT, AN INEVITABLE STAGE

THE SPIRIT LED Jesus into the desert to be tempted by the devil. In the same way a ship leaves the harbor with a set course, Jesus was sent to the desert with a specific purpose and plan. Jesus was led by the Holy Spirit, who was in charge of conceiving Him in Mary's womb, of anointing Him in the Jordan River, of constantly being with Him, of strengthening Him on the cross, and of resurrecting and glorifying Him.

55

The Holy Spirit did the same thing with me. After touching me so deeply, He led me to the desert. Everybody told me to launch out into an evangelistic ministry. Although the anointing and the signs were present, I wasn't ready. So the Spirit led me into a desert.

The desert of the Spirit is not a dry place or a time when God abandons us. Many think they are going through the desert because they don't feel the presence of God in their lives, and they have lost the vitality of that relationship. No! In the deserts of the Spirit, God is real, glorious, and awesome. In the desert of Sinai, Israel had shade by day, fire by night, manna, and quails. There, the presence of God was constantly manifesting. In the deserts prepared by the Spirit, the presence of God is intimate, rich, and intense. However, these experiences always come after a deep touch of the Spirit.

After salvation, the Holy Spirit begins to touch our lives with burdens and callings. Many have felt that touch, that inner voice, which motivates us to serve God, to believe in the impossible, to desire the unreachable. The Spirit puts those desires in our hearts.

Then, what? What do we do with the desire and vision to serve the Lord? What do we do with the deep and sure conviction that God will perform that miracle in our life? What do we do after hearing a powerful message, after an anointed ministry that causes us to rise beyond the impossible and introduces us to the faith to believe God will perform the miracle?

Our parents used to take us to the youth camp sponsored by our denomination every year. The camp lasted a week and usually took place in the mountains beside clear, flowing rivers. There, several hundreds of young Christians would come together to enjoy a week of fellowship, rest, and healthy entertainment. They received the ministry of the Word.

There God dealt with my life. During those weeks of intense ministry, almost everyone attending was sure God was calling him or her to serve Him in one ministry or another.

However, when we returned to our local churches, it was very difficult to materialize that "calling." Generally, the leaders who counseled us would say the same thing: "Wait; God is going to open a door."

What do we do when God lets us know that He has a specific purpose for our lives? The answer is: "Don't do anything; wait." The Holy Spirit, without your request, will lead you into a desert to examine you.

And that's the way it is in the desert of the Spirit. There our vision, our mission, and our faith are tested. In the desert, the heart and the intentions are tested. Don't forget, the Spirit is leading you! The tempter will come because the Holy Spirit allows it to happen. The tempter is a tool in the hands of the Spirit for your benefit.

The Spirit led Jesus into the desert after His experience by the Jordan River to teach Him the power of the Word of God and to allow Him to experience the power that came out of His mouth whenever He said, "It is written." Jesus didn't defeat Satan with experiences—He defeated him with the Word of God.

Frequently, the weapon the devil uses is a deceitful question. He asked Eve: "Did God really say, 'You must not eat from any tree in the garden'?" (Gen. 3:1). To Jesus he said: "If you are the Son of God, tell these stones to become bread" (Matt. 4:3). In the desert of the Spirit, after having been touched by God, the tempter will come to us and ask: "This experience you just had, is it real? Can you trust God? The things you expect of God, will they happen? God probably did it for others, but He will not do it for you."

When Satan confronted Jesus with his deceitful questions, Jesus responded:

> It is written: "Man does not live on bread alone, but on every word that comes from the mouth of God."
> —MATTHEW 4:4

Satan questioned the nature of Jesus as the Son of God. Probably others would have answered him: "Didn't you hear, Satan, what my Father just told me? Don't you remember that in the Jordan He said that I was His son and that He was very pleased with me?"

Not Jesus! Jesus did not defeat the tempter by recounting experiences. He defeated him with the Word, with "IT IS WRITTEN." In the desert of the Spirit, we learn not to depend on our experiences, no matter how glorious they've been, but to live on every word that comes from the mouth of God.

Three times Christ declared, "IT IS WRITTEN." Three times Satan ran away.

In the desert of the Spirit, I learned to lean on the Word of God, not on the experience of that glorious night when I was powerfully touched.

You have probably been tempted by the devil in the same way. You may have questioned your relationship with God, your salvation, your calling, your vision, and your faith. In moments of extreme need, the tempter may have told you God will never perform that miracle for which you are waiting. The tempter will quote the Bible to accuse you. He will do whatever he can to prevent you from relying on the Word.

After several weeks in that desert of learning, one weekend my wife and I decided to go and visit my in-laws, who live in Maryland. When we arrived at their home, we found my mother-in-law in very bad shape. She had been diagnosed with skin cancer.

The type of cancer she had was incurable. The doctors were trying to burn the cancerous cells in the skin with ultraviolet rays. My mother-in-law's face was covered with horrible ulcers, many of them already infected. My wife started to cry. I felt terrible. When I looked into my mother-in-law's eyes, I noticed a profound desperation. I felt that she was asking me for help.

The next day I sat in their living room, talking to one of

my wife's uncles about what was happening to me and how the Holy Spirit was renewing me in the desert. Suddenly, I felt the Holy Spirit touching me from behind; He wanted to do something—the time to pray for my mother-in-law had come.

I ran to the kitchen and told those who were there that we were going to have a little worship service. I put praise and worship music on. The whole family knelt down, and we started to honor the Lord. I knew I had to pray for my mother-in-law, who had an incurable cancer. I understood this was what the Holy Spirit was telling me to do.

However...I also knew I had never prayed for someone with cancer. God had not used me in healing yet. If nothing happened, I was going to be ashamed. I was praying for a family member, not for someone I didn't know. I would not be able to run away.

After worshiping and exalting God and offering myself to Him, I felt the impulse to lay my hands on her and ask for healing. At that moment, she collapsed on the floor. When she got up, she confessed immediately she was healed, even though the ulcers on her skin were still there. That afternoon, God healed my mother-in-law. The next day in a church meeting, she affirmed that God had healed her. After several medical examinations, the doctors who had treated her declared her totally healed from cancer. God had performed the miracle.

Those were moments of testing. If I had based my response on my experiences, I would have been defeated. At these moments one learns to use the Word that comes from the mouth of God. He is my healer, even though He has never used me in healing. God is my healer even when He has never healed me before. God is my provider even though I have never seen that provision. God is my life even if I'm dying. In the desert, we learn to use the Word, not experiences. We learn to see *Him* without looking for signs, confirmations, or evidences. He is faithful.

Sometimes the tempter uses another technique: incitement

to untimely action. He employed it with Jesus, and he will employ it with us. Satan offered Jesus all the kingdoms of the world. Jesus knew all those kingdoms belonged to Him. He was the Creator, the Lord and God of all creation. It wasn't the time, however, to recover them. He had to die first. Satan wanted Jesus to recover the kingdoms of the world without having to go through the cross, without having to experience death, without having to pay for our sins. Doesn't the tempter do the same thing with us? Doesn't he tempt us to make aggressive decisions based on spiritual experiences?

THE MOST DEFIANT DESERT

IN JOHN 13, Jesus prepares Himself to enter into the most important desert of His life: the betrayal by one of His own, His arrest, His cruel suffering at the hands of His executioners, and finally, the Crucifixion.

John starts by saying that Jesus knew "the time had come" (v. 1). After the devil's temptation, several popular ministry crusades, and His own disciples declaring Him king of Israel, Jesus knew His Father's time had come. In verse 3, John declares that Jesus knew the Father had put all things under His power. He had come from the Father and was returning to the Father after accomplishing the mission entrusted to Him. Jesus understood His future clearly. That's why He was willing to go through the desert of Judas' betrayal, through the garden of Gethsemane, the beatings, the crown of thorns, the scorn, the shame, and the death on the cross.

Jesus wanted to prepare His disciples. In verses 31 and 32, He declares the experience that awaited Him would glorify the Son of Man; God also would be glorified. He was entering the desert of the shadow of death. In this desert, He would be alone. No one could enter into it with Him. In verse 33, Jesus tells His disciples that where He was going, they could not come. They weren't ready for it.

Peter didn't like this. He didn't want to leave Jesus alone. Peter was always the first one to react, to speak, and to dare to do what others feared. In verse 36, he asked Jesus, "Lord, where are You going?"

I'm sure that, with all his heart, Peter was ready to follow Jesus wherever He went. However, Jesus knew Peter's heart wasn't ready yet to enter the desert where He was going. That's why Jesus answered him by saying, "Where I am going, you cannot follow now, but you will follow later" (v. 36).

In verse 37, Peter asked Him, "Lord, why can't I follow you now? I will lay down my life for you."

Jesus responded, "I tell you the truth, before the rooster crows, you will disown me three times!" (v. 38).

Jesus finally declared, "Do not let your hearts be troubled. Trust in God; trust also in me" (John 14:1).

Peter wanted to follow Jesus to the desert of death without preparation, without temptation, without having to go through the testing of his faith. He thought he was ready, but Jesus knew he still needed to be tested and tried. Peter's desert experience would come later, after he denied Jesus three times. But Peter would come out of the desert strengthened and assured. He was going to be filled with the Holy Spirit and would become the leader of the early church. But here, in this emotional moment of his denial, he wasn't able to resist. He needed to be tested.

Although the disciples would all go through their desert experiences, the words of Christ ultimately were going to be fulfilled. Jesus promised His disciples they would follow later where He was going. Yes, they would follow Jesus through the desert of suffering, of death—and of victory. When going through their deserts, none of the disciples disowned Him; they were faithful till the end. Historical tradition tells us that all of them, with the exception of John, died as martyrs.

RENEW ME

THE WARMTH OF GOD'S SHELTER

IN THE DESERT of the Spirit, we learn to seek God and only Him. When I was seeking God for His benefits, my prayer was a constant supplication. Sometimes in our prayer times, the presence of God is experienced all around us. We feel good; God is ministering to us. His presence becomes real in our lives. But after a while, that presence leaves, and we don't feel good anymore.

We may feel unworthy of His wonderful presence. Why are God's touches always sudden and so brief? Why aren't they long lasting and intense? Because His touch is meant only to awaken us. It's a warning, an impulse to run after Him to receive more. Without that initial touch, we could not seek Him. We would not know what to seek and what to long for.

When He touches us with His presence and His glory, we know what we have to obtain. We have already experienced the warmth and sweetness of the "shelter of the Most High." His touch triggers our hunger and a longing to be near Him. That was my decision. The touch of God in that crusade was the first step. The manifestations that followed in the radio studio were given to stir up my hunger. As I waited for strength, direction, and instruction in God's presence every morning, I was renewed in my spiritual life. I wasn't interested in my ministry or in the anointing to minister to others. I was interested in the change He was producing *in me*. I was learning new things.

I remember when I used to read my Bible before God's touch upon my life. I preferred the letters of Paul; I thought they were deep and difficult to understand. The psalms I believed to be simple and moving. However, now the psalms were impacting me tremendously. In Psalm 63, in the midst of a very serious situation of life and death, David said these words: "O God, you are my God" (v. 1).

Most people will say they believe in God if you ask them. But if you ask those same people if God is their *per-*

sonal God, very few will answer in an affirmative way. David confessed that God, *Elohim,* the Creator, was his personal God—individual, intimate, close, and well known.

It is obvious from reading the psalms that David knew God intimately. He said, "Earnestly I seek you" (v. 1). He had familiarity with Him. This is achieved when experiences, dialogues, time, joys, pains, and life itself are shared.

The word *earnestly*—literally "at dawn," "in the morning" ("early" in the King James Version)—means more than just a specific time in the morning. *Earnestly* means "first hour, first opportunity." David longed to meet with God at the first opportunity he had. That encounter with God was his priority.

Is meeting with God our first action of the day? When we are facing a difficult situation, is seeking God's presence, His holy direction, our very first response?

Why did David want to seek God? Because his soul was thirsty and his body longed to have communion with God. He had seen God in the sanctuary, in the temple in Jerusalem. David was a worshiper; he knew how to contemplate God in His glorious presence. However, when he wrote Psalm 63, he was in a dry and weary land, without water, and without any protection. He was in a desert. David needed to seek and find his God.

GOD DOESN'T ABANDON US

IN PSALM 63:8, DAVID said, "My soul clings to you."

The word *cling* means "to procure, to adhere, to follow closely, and to reach." David was procuring God. He wanted to be very close to Him. This is how God deals with us. First He comes close, invites us, attracts us, and touches us. Then it seems that He leaves and moves away. Why?

He does it to see if we will run after Him, if we will seek Him. How many are satisfied by a simple experience! After a touch of God, the Holy Spirit puts us in deserts to learn to know God and the power of His Word. There we learn to seek Him, to thirst for Him, to long for Him over everything else.

David concludes Psalm 63 by saying:

> But the king will rejoice in God; all who swear by God's name will praise him, while the mouths of liars will be silenced.
>
> —VERSE 11

God will take care of the enemies of those who seek Him in the desert and who allow the Holy Spirit to lead them into dry lands. Therefore, I didn't worry about my future, about the things I could "do" for God. My desire has been, and still is, to know Him, to find Him, to rejoice in Him, and to be transformed every day from glory to glory into His image. The rest will come in God's time.

Have you ever doubted that God would fulfill His promise to you? Have you ever wondered why God takes so long to answer? Have you tried to "help" God? Have you made decisions before God's time? Do you feel guilty? Allow me to tell you that Christ understands you.

Jesus appeared to His disciples in the most painful and depressing moment of their lives. They were hiding, filled with fear and cowardice. Peter felt like the biggest traitor in the world. Three times he had denied his Lord. But when Jesus appeared to His disciples, He breathed on them, anointed them with the Holy Spirit, and sent them to wait together until the Holy Spirit filled them with power from above. Many times I have asked myself why Jesus breathed on them. Jesus knew the Holy Spirit was going to fill them on the Day of Pentecost. This earlier moment was not the fullness of Pentecost.

To be filled with the Holy Spirit in the upper room on the Day of Pentecost, they had to be together, unanimous, and prepared. They never would have achieved this in their own strength. I'm sure they would have fought and blamed each other for Jesus' death. I'm sure they would have started to compare themselves with each other. But Jesus appeared and anointed them with the power of the Holy Spirit to keep them united, focused on God's will, focused on God's promise, and waiting for the fullness of the Holy Spirit.

Jesus will do exactly the same thing in your life. When the Spirit leads you into a desert of rejection, loneliness, loss, and difficulty, do not despair. Do not think God has left you, that you are being punished. In the worst moment, Jesus will come to breathe strength. Trust in Him. Wait in Him. His breath of strength will empower you to patiently stay in your desert until His work is accomplished.

Six

DISCIPLE INSTEAD OF FOLLOWER

THE HOLY SPIRIT took direct control of my spiritual life. You may be wondering what was happening previously in my spiritual life. I have no doubt that He was working in me, but I was also working. I was in control of my spiritual life, of my religious activities, and of my service to the Lord. Even though I was serving Him with all my heart, I was doing it with my own human strength. When I recognized I couldn't please God with my own human efforts and surrendered, the Holy Spirit started to renew me and take me to new places, new experiences, and the relationship with God I had always dreamed about.

The same thing that had happened to Simon Peter the fisherman was happening to me. One day, he saw a big crowd following a man called *Jesus of Nazareth* (Luke 5). The people were "crowding" around Him to listen to the Word of God. When Jesus saw such a big crowd, He decided to teach from one of the boats that stood at the water's edge. The boat belonged to Peter, who used it to make a living. Peter had been fishing all night and had applied all the fishing skills necessary to obtain an abundance of fish, but he hadn't been successful. "Put out into deep water, and let down the nets for a catch," commanded Jesus (Luke 5:4).

When Peter obeyed, the nets broke because of the large number of fish. What a miracle! Peter was astounded. When they went back to the shore, he recognized the authority of Jesus. Falling on his knees he said, "Go away from me, Lord; I am a sinful man" (v. 8).

Why did he say those words? Did Peter recognize his own sinful nature? Did he repent from all his sins? I don't think so. See what the next two verses say:

> For he and all his companions were astonished at the catch of fish they had taken, and so were James and John, the sons of Zebedee, Simon's partners.
> —LUKE 5:9–10

At that moment, Jesus called Peter, and from then on, Peter followed Jesus. He witnessed the fishing miracle. He saw the God of nature in action, and he saw the preacher of the kingdom of God. He met with the Messiah, the Savior. When he saw the Lord, he decided to follow Him. But he did it as a "follower," not as a true disciple. He was a devout follower, but not a disciple.

Peter wanted to follow the Lord. He was even ready to lay down his life for Him. But Jesus didn't accept the sacrifice. (See John 13:37–38.) In that moment, the sacrifice of Peter's life had no spiritual value. Peter was doing it out of devotion, love, and faithfulness to an ideal. But Jesus didn't want this offering. Peter was only following Jesus. He had to learn to be a true disciple.

When did he learn? He learned after having denied Jesus. After having failed. After realizing that to be more aggressive or loyal was not enough. He had to go through the disappointment, the pain, and the betrayal of his own heart. Peter disowned Jesus three times. He denied his Teacher, the One who had loved him, taught him, and blessed him so many times. Imagine the pain Peter must have experienced when he saw Christ on the cross and when he saw Him laid in the tomb. Imagine his remorse every night when, closing his eyes, he remembered how he had betrayed his Lord.

However, one day after that bitter experience, Jesus met Peter by the Sea of Galilee. He found him weak, hopeless, and meek. Jesus didn't hold the betrayal against him. He simply called him to feed His lambs. Jesus said to Peter, "Follow me!" (John 21:19).

When Peter heard those words, he looked at John, the disciple whom Jesus loved, the model disciple, the one who had been faithful until the end. "Lord, what about him?" Peter asked (v. 21). He probably thought John was the one who would be put in charge of the sheep.

Jesus' answer was like a clap of thunder: "What is that to you? You must follow me" (v. 22). Peter was now prepared. He had passed through the desert of testing. He realized he couldn't follow the Lord with the strength of his determination. He had to be a disciple.

What does it mean to follow Jesus? To be His disciple? How do we become His disciples? By carrying out what He said:

> Then he called the crowd to him along with his disciples and said: "If anyone would come after me, he must deny himself and take up his cross and follow me. For whoever wants to save his life will lose it, but whoever loses his life for me and for the gospel will save it."
>
> —MARK 8:34–35

SELF-DENIAL

WE BECOME DISCIPLES by denying ourselves. To deny oneself is to live knowing that my ego will always be an enemy of the will of Jesus Christ. It is to live fully conscious of the interest of Christ, not fulfilling my own interests, goals, and opinions. It is to be aware of the will and desires of the Lord Jesus.

In this desert of renewal, the Holy Spirit transformed my prayer life, worship, praise, study of the Word, and ministry. I used to worship, pray, study the Bible, and minister as I had been taught and in the best way I could according to my human efforts. I had been taught that in order to please God one has to sacrifice, to "pay the price." I thought paying the price was simply doing something against my will. I thought whenever I did something that was hard for me to do, something I didn't like to do, God was pleased. So, when I wanted to sleep, I would wake up to pray. But it was a forced prayer.

Throughout history, many religious people have done the same thing in convents, monasteries, and caves. In those cold and gloomy places, these religious people have tried to please God by praying many hours a day in very uncomfortable positions, fasting, and making vows of poverty and silence.

Even though I never reached that point, my motivation was the same. I prayed because it was my duty. I worshiped God because He is worthy, although I didn't do it sincerely. I imagine how my father would feel if he were to discover that I love him because it is my obligation to love and honor him who conceived me, raised me, and gave me his name. I believe my father would not reject me, but he would feel very hurt and offended.

WHEN GOD ASKS, GIVE HIM

ABRAHAM RECEIVED REVELATION from God after the original promise was fulfilled. God had promised him two things: descendants and territory. At the beginning of his journey of faith, God showed him the land he was going to possess and allowed him to live in it. But Abraham lived there like a stranger, in a tent surrounded by Canaanites.

Toward the end of his life, Abraham had a son called Isaac. He could finally breathe with a little less anxiety: God had fulfilled His promise. Apparently, Abraham was now done. Sarah was happy because she had finally been able to conceive, and Isaac was rich and prosperous as a young man. "And they lived happily ever after." No way! Abraham needed renewal. He needed to know God in a different dimension.

One day, God tested Abraham. In Genesis 22:1, He called him by name: "Abraham!" Abraham knew that voice already. God didn't have to use a lot of words to get his attention.

When Abraham heard his name, he simply answered, "Here I am" (v. 1). What surrender! What an attitude! He was ready to do whatever God asked of him, with no exceptions, no prejudices, and no limitations. The answer of the heart came quickly: "Lord, I'm at your disposal."

When we surrender to God like that, we open our hearts for Him to take us from glory to glory, from renewal to renewal. But now comes the difficult part. When God brings us to the place of renewal, to the place of revelation, to the place of anointing, He asks something of us.

God asked of Abraham two things. First, He told him to go the region of Moriah, to an unknown mountain that God in His time was going to show him. Secondly, He told him to take his beloved son Isaac and to sacrifice him there on an altar. Abraham didn't doubt God. In verse 3, it says that he got up early the next morning and left toward Moriah in obedience to God.

First, God directs Abraham toward Moriah. He told him to leave the comfort of his family, friends, employees, and tent to travel to a mountainous place, deserted and unknown. He had never been there; it was a new place for him.

Abraham had to go through this experience alone. This is God's way. In order to go to a new place, God tells us to leave the comfortable, the familiar, and the known. To receive something new from God, we need to hand Him something old.

During these last few months, I have talked to many people who sincerely desire to be renewed. However, I find rejection when I start to explain to them that they have to be willing to change, to give up certain habits, certain mentalities, and certain routines. Today, for example, many resist change, criticizing Christian music and different styles of worship such as using dance, playing the tambourine, and displaying banners. Others criticize the different manifestations of power, such as emotional expressions, charismatic gifts, laughter, shaking, falling, dreams, and visions.

I know it is very difficult to change. However, it is necessary to surrender whatever disturbs the work of renewal of the Holy Spirit—even our resistance to change.

Have you ever asked God, "Lord, what are You doing in my life?" I have asked Him this question many times. Abraham didn't ask Him for any explanations, though; he simply got up early, took his son, and started the journey.

If you have ever wondered what God is doing in your life, don't wait for Him to tell you. God doesn't explain *what He does,* but He wants to reveal *who He is.* He didn't explain to Abraham what He was going to do with him and with Isaac. Yet God was going to reveal one of His names to Abraham: *Jehovah-Jireh,* the provider. God wanted to renew the original covenant, and then He wanted to add some additional blessings to it.

Abraham went to Moriah. He knew the territory, but he didn't know the place in the mountain that God had prepared for the sacrifice. The path of renewal is a path of dependence on the Holy Spirit's direction. He is the only one who knows how He is going to renew us, when He will do it, and where. We can't tell God to renew us in a particular area but not in another. He directs us; we must simply trust.

When Abraham arrived at the mountain God had shown him, he went up and began to prepare Isaac for the sacrifice. God had given Isaac to him in a miraculous way, but now He was demanding him back! In the place of renewal, where God reveals new aspects of His character to us, He demands sacrifice. What sacrifices does He want? He wants all those things that bind us, control us, and keep us from having a heart completely surrendered to Him. In Abraham's case, God asked him to give Him his beloved son Isaac. What is God asking you to sacrifice? Is there anything in your life that occupies your thoughts all the time? Is there anything that dominates and controls your decisions? Are there concepts or ideas that determine your perception of God and His kingdom?

God doesn't need our sacrifices. God didn't need Isaac. However, God wanted Abraham to have a free heart, without bondages, totally dependent on Him. When God demands us to sacrifice something that binds us, He wants to free us from the things that don't allow us to see Him as He truly is. How many customs, traditions, and old-fashioned experiences disturb our hearts? How many denominational prides blind our hearts to an authentic renewing revelation of God?

Many times I hear from frustrated Christians who want to break all their bondages so they can experience new dimensions of the person of Christ as revealed by the Holy Spirit. But there are obstacles. One of the most common is: "What will my circle of friends and my leaders say?" I have spoken with many who have confessed a hunger for renewal, but they are afraid the people in their church group will label them as fanatics, strange, liberals, charismatics, and other names that would tarnish their reputations. I have heard several people declare they do not believe in many of the traditions, but they endure and suffer because they are afraid of being rejected or branded. On the altar of renewal, God will ask us to sacrifice those fears and burdens that get in the way.

Abraham obeyed; he didn't want any barriers. I also obeyed; in the most critical moments of my desert, God asked me to sacrifice two things: my reputation and my ministry.

I come from a traditional Italian family. In European culture, as well as in our Latin American culture, the family's reputation and good name are protected. I have always been careful not to stain my family's name through any dishonest action. However, there were people who were tarnishing my name and reputation. I had to surrender until I was able to accept that if my name were destroyed, I would still trust in the Lord and not run away from my responsibilities or God's plan for my life.

Since early childhood, I have been sure of God's calling on my life; I knew I was going to be a minister of the Lord. My very identity was based upon the fact that God was calling me to be a minister. Therefore, my whole life was designed toward that goal. I never thought about the possibility of another career. However, in the Holy Spirit's desert, God asked for my ministry, for my identity. I had to give it to Him and be ready to be anything. I was set free. I lost my fear of those who were planning my destruction. What were they going to destroy? All the things they could hurt—my name and my ministry—were already dead in the hands of God from the moment I gave them to Him. Satan had nothing else to do.

The questions I feared the most disappeared: *What will they say? What will they think? Are they going to accept me? Will they believe the lies launched against me? Where will I go if they don't want me here anymore? It will be a scandal!* I was set free from them all.

Isaac didn't belong to Abraham but to God. Our talents don't belong to us either. Our ministry is not ours. The church is not ours. The family, earthly goods, career, plans—none are ours. Neither are we the owners of our reputations. Our lives belong to God. On the altar of renewal, in the desert of the Spirit, God will ask us to sacrifice what worries us the most, that which holds us in bondage. Before He begins renewal, God wants a heart free from every bondage, no matter how good and "spiritual" it may be. God doesn't want anything to stop us from "knowing the Lord," from listening to His voice.

We can spend our lives doing God's work and never come to know the Lord. A pastor once told me that after praying to present all the needs of his church, his council, and his family before God, he had no time left to listen to God's voice.

THE SONS OF ZERUIAH

KING DAVID WAS anointed to build the kingdom of Israel. We read that God gave him an army to fight the battles to establish the kingdom of Israel. In the army that helped David were three men called "the sons of Zeruiah."

Who were the sons of Zeruiah? In 1 Chronicles 2:13–16, David's genealogy shows us that Zeruiah was David's sister and that her sons were Abishai, Joab, and Asahel. These three men were not only generals in David's army but also his nephews. Yet, in 2 Samuel 19:22, David called them "adversaries."

Joab was a courageous man. He conquered the city of Zion, and David appointed him general. Joab built David's kingdom.

When Joab conquered a city called Rabbah, before entering in to take the city and have total dominion over it, he called David (2 Sam. 12:26). The conquest would then be the king's, and the city named after David, not after Joab. He was a loyal man and fought the king's battles. When David commanded that a census be taken of Israel, Joab tried to convince him not to commit that sin. Joab was protecting David from sin. When David was concerned for Absalom, Joab managed to bring him to David so the king would be happy. Joab enjoyed the king's happiness.

Abishai, his brother, was also a valiant man in battle. When David came into the cave where Saul was sleeping, Abishai wanted to kill Saul. After all, Saul had been trying to kill David.

On one occasion, David tired while fighting against a giant, and he almost lost his life. Abishai confronted the giant and killed him. That day, Abishai swore that they were going to protect the king and would not let him fight anymore. Abishai would give his life for his king.

What brave, loyal, and faithful men these sons of Zeruiah were. They fought the king's battles and built David's kingdom. Why, then, did David call them adversaries?

One day, David had to run away from Jerusalem because his son Absalom had usurped the throne. As he was leaving, a man named Shimei insulted David. When Abishai heard him, he immediately suggested that this man die because he had cursed the Lord's anointed. It is in the midst of this situation that David called the sons of Zeruiah "adversaries."

Joab and Abishai did not understand David, who would cry when his enemies died. When Joab killed Abner, Saul's general and the one in charge of capturing David by Saul's orders, David cried and wouldn't eat. David had mercy for his son Absalom and ordered his men not to kill him, even though Absalom was trying to kill him. At his first chance, when Joab found Absalom hanging from a tree, he killed him. David cried bitterly over the death of Absalom, but Joab never understood.

Even though these men were loyal, courageous, and faithful, David referred to them as "adversaries." Even though they fought for the king, served him, and built the kingdom, they didn't have the king's heart. We can be the best workers in the church, making enormous sacrifices, but if we don't have our King's heart, we become His adversaries.

We can, like Peter, be willing to give our lives for the Lord and His cause. In Mark 8, Jesus speaks very clearly about His sufferings and death at the hands of the Jewish religious leaders. In verse 32, Mark says: "He spoke plainly about this, and Peter took him aside and began to rebuke him." The word *rebuke* means "to scold severely." Jesus reacted to Peter's words by saying:

> Get behind me, Satan! . . . You do not have in mind the
> things of God, but the things of men.
>
> —MARK 8:33

With the best of intentions, Peter rebuked Jesus. He didn't want the religious leaders to mistreat Jesus. But that was a carnal and human desire. Peter became an enemy, an adversary of Jesus. When a Christian tries to please God with his carnal desires, his mental abilities, or his human talents, he opposes the purposes of God; Satan then comes on the scene and frustrates God's revelation in the person's life.

When Peter understood that he had failed, that he had denied Christ, Jesus came and anointed him with the Holy Spirit. He also anointed me with the Holy Spirit when I realized I was never going to be able to please God with my own efforts, my religious prayer exercises, my fasting, my theological studies, and my work in the church.

Joab had a sad ending. On his deathbed, David leaves instructions for his son Solomon regarding the sons of Zeruiah. They had to be killed. Solomon, carrying out his father's will, sent soldiers to kill Joab, but Joab sought refuge in the tabernacle and took hold of the horns of the altar. To take hold of the horns of the altar was to ask for mercy. When Solomon was informed that Joab had entered the holy of holies to stand before the altar, he ordered that he be executed without mercy.

The altar of sacrifice with its horns is a symbol of the cross of Jesus Christ. How many are taking hold of the cross but don't have the heart of the "Crucified"? Are you a son of Zeruiah, an adversary of God's purposes in the earth, in His church, in your family, and in your life? You can be an excellent Christian whose salvation is sure. However, if you don't have God's heart, you won't be an instrument of blessing, transformation, and renewal.

When one takes off the mask of a good Christian and stops living a life of deceit, the promises of Jesus to

Nathanael are fulfilled in the believer's life also:

> I tell you the truth, you shall see heaven open, and the angels of God ascending and descending on the Son of Man.
>
> —JOHN 1:51

THE COVENANT RENEWED

THIS SAME THING happened in Abraham's life. In the very moment he lifted the knife to sacrifice Isaac, something wonderful happened. The heavens opened, and God spoke. The angel of the Lord said, "Abraham! Abraham! . . . Do not lay a hand on the boy. . . . Do not do anything to him. Now I know that you fear God, because you have not withheld from me your son, your only son" (Gen. 22:11–12).

The angel declared that Abraham had been examined and his heart was free from all bondage. Abraham was not bound to the "promise," to Isaac. He was bound to God. His heart was not concerned about "his descendants"; he was concerned about God. My heart stopped being concerned about the ministry, the calling, and my reputation. My heart became attached to God.

After Abraham passed God's test, the covenant was renewed. The original covenant according to Genesis 12 had been as follows:

> I will make you into a great nation and I will bless you; I will make your name great, and you will be a blessing. I will bless those who bless you, and whoever curses you I will curse; and all peoples on earth will be blessed through you.
>
> —GENESIS 12:2–3

In Genesis 22, God renews the covenant by adding some additional promises:

> Your descendants will take possession of the cities of
> their enemies, and through your offspring all nations
> on earth will be blessed, because you have obeyed me.
> —GENESIS 22:17–18

Notice the difference. After Abraham surrendered to God
in total obedience by giving Him everything, God promised
him that he would not only be a blessing to his nation, but
that his offspring would bless all nations on earth as well.
God promised not only to curse those who cursed him, but
He was also going to give his descendants cities, possessions, and authority over his enemies.

Every time a man or a woman surrenders like this, the
heavens open, God reveals Himself, provides the sacrifice
that is truly pleasing to Him, and promises victory over the
enemy. Abraham's true sacrifice wasn't Isaac, but his love,
his dependence, and his total confidence in God. On that
altar, Abraham came to know the God who provides,
Jehovah-Jireh. This name literally means "I AM (*Jehovah*)
will be seen (*Jireh*)." Abraham received the revelation of the
"I AM" who would be present in every moment of need.
When we can't solve problems with our own abilities, when
we reach the end of all possibilities, God appears and provides. He will reveal Himself.

If you go to Jerusalem, you will see that the mountain
where Abraham offered Isaac is only a few meters away
from Calvary. In those same hills, God the Father "broke"
His Son Jesus on the cross for us. Our sacrifices could not
attain forgiveness. The Father provided the innocent Lamb
of God to be sacrificed on that Passover day, and so
destroyed the gates of the enemy—death.

In short, our sacrifices are not enough. Our efforts are not
sufficient. When we surrender, He provides the true sacrifice, one that is pleasing. We can affirm the following:

- When we offer *our pride* as a sacrifice to Him, He lifts
  our head and gives the gates of our enemies to us.

- When we offer *our talents* as a sacrifice to Him, He acts according to the power that is working in us.
- When we offer *our fears* as a sacrifice to Him, He comforts us and gives us faith.
- When we offer *our ministries* as a sacrifice to Him, He teaches us to be humble disciples.
- When we offer *our reputation* as a sacrifice to Him, He is our glory.
- When we offer *our possessions* as a sacrifice to Him, He is our provider and supplier.
- When we offer *our words* as a sacrifice to Him, He imparts His Word to us.
- When we offer *our lives* as sacrifices to Him, He gives His life to us.
- When we offer *our names* as sacrifices to Him, He gives us His own.
- When we offer *our hearts* as sacrifices to Him, He gives His heart to us.
- When we offer *our devotion* as a sacrifice to Him, He teaches us to worship Him in spirit and in truth.

WHEN HEAVEN OPENS

THE BIBLE SAYS that when we stop trying to achieve God's favor, the heavens open. God then reveals His power and provides, prospers, guides, comforts, resurrects, defeats the enemy, and glorifies Himself.

Isaac saw the heavens open in his life. He was a man who feared God, but he needed to be renewed. Even though he knew God and had heard His voice, he still depended on his own human tricks. While he was living in Gerar, God spoke to him and promised him protection and blessing according to the oath He had sworn to his father, Abraham. But when the moment of faith arrived, and the men in the region started to investigate who Rebekah was, Isaac lied by saying she was his sister. He was afraid they would take Rebekah and kill him. And God's promise? Isaac forgot all about it. (See Genesis 26:6–11.)

When he had to leave Gerar because he had prospered much and his neighbors were jealous, Isaac left without complaining and settled in the valley. There he lived and found the wells that his father Abraham had dug. Even though he had failed, God prospered him. (See Genesis 26:17–19.) That was the beginning of his renewal.

When some herdsmen demanded those wells, Isaac didn't quarrel. When some other herdsmen wanted the new well he had dug, he looked for another. Isaac didn't quarrel. He kept on looking until he found the well he wanted, and then he named it *Rehoboth* (Genesis 26:22). After this test of meekness:

> That night the LORD appeared to him and said, "I am the God of your father Abraham. Do not be afraid, for I am with you; I will bless you and will increase the number of your descendants for the sake of my servant Abraham." Isaac built an altar there and called on the name of the LORD. There he pitched his tent, and there his servants dug a well.
> —GENESIS 26:24–25

When the men that hated Isaac saw his renewal, they told him:

> We saw clearly that the LORD was with you; so we said, "There ought to be a sworn agreement between us"— between us and you. Let us make a treaty with you that you will do us no harm, just as we did not molest you but always treated you well and sent you away in peace. And now you are blessed by the LORD.
> —GENESIS 26:28–29

Heaven opened, Isaac prospered in peace, and even his neighbors saw God was with him. He didn't have to convince anyone, he didn't have to negotiate, and he didn't have to deceive anyone with lies. They honored him.

Jacob had a similar experience. God sent him back to the land of his ancestors, to the place where he belonged. But there was a problem. He had to reconcile with his brother, Esau, whom he had cheated and deceived. He had no more tricks available. He had reached the limit of his abilities. He needed God's blessing. In a place called *Peniel,* God opened the heavens, and Jacob was changed forever. In that place, Jacob wrestled with God. He knew he couldn't face the future without God's blessing, so he wrestled until he got it. He was desperate to obtain God's renewing touch. What a beautiful anxiety! (See Genesis 32.)

When God asked him what his name was, Jacob had to confess that his name was *Deceiver.* Seeing this man's humiliation, God renewed and transformed him. When Jacob met Esau, he wasn't the "deceiver" anymore, but *Israel,* "he who struggles with God and with men and has overcome." The old Jacob had died. He had been renewed.

God also opened the heavens in the life of Joseph. During his time in jail, Joseph tried to be set free. There he became a friend with Pharaoh's cupbearer. After he interpreted the cupbearer's dream, Joseph told him:

> But when all goes well with you, remember me and show me kindness; mention me to Pharaoh and get me out of this prison.
>
> —GENESIS 40:14

Joseph trusted this man. However, the Bible says that the cupbearer didn't remember Joseph (Gen. 40:23). How sad! This is how many of our dreams end. Joseph didn't try to negotiate his freedom. He had to endure two more years in prison.

However, God didn't forget him. When Pharaoh had a dream, the heavens opened. God revealed to Joseph the interpretation of that dream. In those two years, Joseph had learned to wait on God. After prison—after that desert—the heavens were opened, and God revealed Himself and raised Joseph from the jail to the throne. (See Genesis 41.)

Moses also tried to do God's will with his own strength. He understood that God had called him to free His people from slavery. He had been raised in the Egyptian culture. He was intellectually brilliant, skilled in politics, and physically strong. He trusted his abilities. The first opportunity he had, he killed an Egyptian who was mistreating a Jew. He took justice into his own hands. After all, he was Moses, Pharaoh's daughter's protégé, and future liberator of Israel. (See Exodus 2.)

God had to take him to the desert to renew him. One day, the heavens opened on Mount Horeb and Moses saw a bush on fire that did not burn up. From within the bush, God called to him by name, and he responded, "Here I am" (Exod. 3:4).

In that place, God called him again. However, Moses didn't care about his own ideals or his own interests any longer. The most important things to him were not his name, his talents, or his abilities. The only thing that mattered to him was having divine authority. That's why he wanted to know God's name. And there, in that place of total humiliation, God opened the heavens and revealed His name to him: "I AM WHO I AM." In this way, God gave him an authority based on the revelation of His name.

Something similar happened to Isaiah. When King Uzziah died, and the throne of Israel became vacant—a very bitter period in Isaiah's life—the heavens opened, and the Lord revealed Himself seated on a throne, high and exalted. Isaiah left that place renewed, with a clear message for the people of Israel. (See Isaiah 6.)

When Jesus yielded to His Father's authority by humbling Himself, and John the Baptist baptized Him in fulfillment of the prophecies, the heavens opened and the Holy Spirit and the Father manifested themselves.

When Stephen abandoned his life into God's hands and didn't defend himself when he was condemned to die, the heavens opened and Jesus was revealed to him in a vision. Stephen's face shone, and he faced death without any fear. (See Acts 7.)

Finally, in the last book of the Bible, the heavens opened for John. His apostolic ministry had been triumphant, but he had been confined to the island of Patmos because of the Word of God and the testimony of Jesus. On that abandoned island, he didn't complain or ask God to set him free. Being in the Spirit on the Lord's Day, the heavens opened and he heard a voice, the voice of the First and the Last, the Living One, the One who was dead and now is alive forever and ever, He who holds the keys of death and Hades. He received the revelation of Jesus Christ, the faithful witness, the firstborn from the dead, the Sovereign of all the kings of the earth, He who loved us and cleansed us from all our sins with His blood and made us kings and priests for God, He who comes in the clouds and will be seen by all, the Alpha and the Omega, He who is and who was and who is to come, the almighty Lord. (See Revelation 1.)

When do the heavens open? When there is no deceit. When we stop striving to please God. When we don't try to help God, and when all human plans disappear and only God's plans remain. They open when we surrender, even though we may be:

- In the desert of the Spirit, like Jesus.
- By the altar, sacrificing the only thing we possess, like Abraham.
- In a place surrounded by our enemies, like Isaac.
- Facing someone who is very angry, like Jacob.
- In jail, like Joseph.
- In a desert, like Moses.
- Grieving, like Isaiah.
- On our way to the cross, like Jesus.
- Facing martyrdom, like Stephen.
- Alone and abandoned, like John on Patmos.
- Having failed Jesus, like Peter.

83

The heavens will open, and we will be renewed. God will reveal His person, His glory, in new and fresh ways.

In the place of renewal, God will ask you to give Him whatever is preventing the full revelation of Christ, until He becomes our only desire. Did you notice a common characteristic in all of the renewing experiences we have mentioned? God asks for something, we give Him what He asks, and He gives us a new revelation of Himself. What did all these people give to Him?

- Abraham gave Him his life and the life of his son.
- Isaac gave Him his rights and his goods.
- Jacob gave Him his crisis, deceitful past, and future.
- Joseph gave Him the injustice committed against his life.
- Moses gave Him his name, his talents, and his life.
- Isaiah gave Him the throne of his heart.
- Peter gave Him his human strengths.
- Stephen gave Him his physical life.
- John gave Him his life of isolation on an island.
- Jesus gave Himself through the Holy Spirit.

All these men received revelation from God that transformed their lives. "Therefore," as the writer of the Book of Hebrews says, "since we are surrounded by such a great cloud of witnesses, let us throw off everything that hinders and the sin that so easily entangles, and let us run with perseverance the race marked out for us. Let us fix our eyes on Jesus, the author and perfecter of our faith, who for the joy set before him endured the cross, scorning its shame, and sat down at the right hand of the throne of God" (Heb. 12:1–2). Abraham, Isaac, Jacob, Joseph, Moses, Isaiah, Peter, Stephen, and John are our cloud of witnesses. Now it's our turn to run our race.

To Run, Several Things Need to Be Done

THROW OFF ALL WEIGHT. Weight is mass, fat. It is something with no value. There are activities that don't produce character and don't produce any fruit in our lives. We have to get rid of all weight, all that is fat and useless. Weight may not be sin, but it is a hindrance. It besieges us. If we don't give it away, we will stumble on our way to renewal.

Throw off all sin. There is only one way to do it: Confess. John says in his first letter that if we confess our sins, God is faithful and just in His forgiveness of our sins and in His purification of us from all unrighteousness (1 John 1:9).

Run with our eyes fixed on Jesus; follow His example of surrender. Does this mean we have to lift our eyes to heaven and always be looking up, overlooking our daily responsibilities? No. To fix our eyes on Jesus means to simply believe in Him. It is as Jesus said in John 3:14–15: "Just as Moses lifted up the snake in the desert, so the Son of Man must be lifted up, that everyone who believes in him may have eternal life."

At one time, God asked me to give Him my desire to have "experiences." My desire was to be able to see the spiritual world like many others who say they've seen angels and demons. God told me I didn't have to see angels to know that I had their protection. Doesn't Psalm 91 say that angels guard me in all my ways and lift me up in their hands so my foot will not strike against a stone? I didn't have to see demons to know that our struggle is not against flesh and blood (Eph. 6:12). God showed me that the most important thing is to know He is the Most High, the Omnipotent, according to His Word. When we believe what the Bible says without having to depend on experiences, we fix our eyes on Jesus, the author and perfecter of our faith.

Talk to the Lord. Tell Him you want to be renewed in His revelation. He who knows God is transformed. I knew a lot about Christ, but I didn't have an intimate and personal revelation of Jesus.

You probably have known Jesus as your Savior. He is much more than your Savior and Healer. He is much more than what we understand and ask for. He is much more than experiences. He is much more than what you may have known and experienced. Don't be satisfied with what you've seen, experienced, and learned. Don't be satisfied with what you have achieved. Experience Paul's feeling when he said:

> For this reason I kneel before the Father, from whom his whole family in heaven and on earth derives its name. I pray that out of his glorious riches he may strengthen you with power through his Spirit in your inner being, so that Christ may dwell in your hearts through faith. And I pray that you, being rooted and established in love, may have power, together with all the saints, to grasp how wide and long and high and deep is the love of Christ, and to know this love that surpasses knowledge—that you may be filled to the measure of all the fullness of God.
>
> Now to him who is able to do immeasurably more than all we ask or imagine, according to his power that is at work within us, to him be glory in the church and in Christ Jesus throughout all generations, for ever and ever! Amen.
>
> —EPHESIANS 3:14–21

Seven

ACCORDING TO GOD'S HEART

THAT FRIDAY EVENING at the crusade in Toronto, I sat in the front row of the Maple Leaf Gardens arena, watching intently the man of God on the platform. Even though he was in front of thousands of people, he worshiped God as if he were all alone in his room. I had never seen a preacher worship the way Pastor Benny Hinn was worshiping. I was used to seeing the preacher step up to the pulpit, greet the congregation, and then preach a message. After all, preachers are meant to preach. They generally become the focus of attention.

Thousands of people in the auditorium began to worship with him. At the beginning of the meeting, we were all focused on the preacher and on the expectation of the miracles we were about to witness. However, as the worship service developed, we started to forget where we were. The main purpose of the occasion became honoring and glorifying Christ.

Pastor Benny spent more than an hour worshiping the Lord with his eyes closed and his hands raised. He kept telling us to keep our eyes closed and to worship Christ. The Lord was the only One who mattered in that place.

He gradually introduced us to the manifest presence of

God until we reached His divine throne. For a moment, it seemed as if he had come before Jesus. At that moment, he presented the night's intercession: "Lord, touch those in need!" That is when the confidence, the courage, emerged. At that very moment of absolute trust, Pastor Hinn seemed to be totally sure that whatever he asked before the throne would be granted.

Spectacular physical miracles took place. Many people were delivered from addictions or mental and satanic bondages; others received the anointing of the Holy Spirit. What was the key? What was the door? Why did so many miracles take place? Because there was an anointed declaration of the Word of God in an atmosphere of worship.

In the months that followed, some ministers began to report on the effect that meeting had on their own lives and the ministry in their churches. As these pastors went back to their places of ministry, they began to pray for the sick and adapt their own services to the pattern they had observed in the crusade. They had seen the example of worship. They learned that the purpose of worship was not just so miracles would occur. The purpose of worship was to allow people to come to the place of ultimate surrender to the will of the Holy Spirit. The example I witnessed that night motivated me to become a worshiper. I had seen a man so deeply surrendered to God that he became a helpful instrument in the hands of the miraculous Jesus Christ.

Many times as we ask God for things in prayer, we think we need to convince Him to give them to us. As if we would have to convince Him to bless, to heal, and to deliver! God *wants* to do those things; He doesn't need to be convinced. In our prayers, worship, and communion, God wants us to surrender to Him in such a way that we become manageable vessels, pure and clean, instruments for His glory. I realized I had been practicing the disciplines of prayer, praise, worship, study of the Word of God, and ministry with the intention of achieving certain results. I hadn't been searching God with integrity, purity of heart, or worship directed totally to Him. I needed to repent.

A True Worshiper

MORE THAN HIS way of ministering, more than his style, I was impacted by the way Benny Hinn worshiped the Lord. He surrendered to the will of the Holy Spirit to be used as an instrument of blessing; he guided thousands of people to take their eyes away from their problems and fix them on Christ. The secret of that powerful anointing for the proclamation of the Word of God, for healing and deliverance, is found in surrendered worship at the feet of King Jesus, the miracle-maker. This is the first step: Make it your intention to be a true worshiper, and say to God, "Father, have You been looking for me? Here I am. I want to worship You in spirit and in truth. Teach me."

I left that service determined to become a worshiper. The next day, I began to ask God hundreds of questions. "How am I going to change? What will happen to me?" I felt insecure, but at the same time, full of hope. I had always been aware that God's will for my life contrasted strongly with my flaws and offenses, which I longed to eliminate and overcome. I wanted to develop my talents and my abilities to be a better servant of God. The problem was I never felt I had achieved that.

True Repentance

I HAD TO TAKE a crucial second step toward spiritual renewal: I needed to repent. This is the key that introduces us to the renewal.

What is *repentance?* First, it is a change in the way we think, a change of attitude that produces sadness and pain. This change doesn't transform the heart. It simply produces remorse. Such was the case of Judas:

When Judas, who had betrayed him, saw that Jesus

was condemned, he was seized with remorse and returned the thirty silver coins to the chief priests and the elders.

—MATTHEW 27:3

Judas felt bad when he saw Jesus bound and being handed over to Pilate (Matt. 27:2). His reaction was to commit suicide. His "repentance" didn't change his heart; it simply depressed him and led him to hang himself. To feel bad about something is not true repentance.

Second, repentance is a change of direction after a transforming analysis of behavior, which happens as a result of knowledge. As a consequence, one abandons what is wrong and turns toward what is right.

In the case of renewal, repentance goes beyond remorse, beyond the admission of wrongdoing. There is a change of direction in which one not only moves away from what is opposed to God, but also turns to God. The heart that is renewed not only moves away from sin, self-sufficiency, and pride, but also turns entirely to God. The Bible says that repentance brings the forgiveness of sins and times of renewing in the presence of the Lord.

> Repent, then, and turn to God, so that your sins may
> be wiped out, that times of refreshing may come from
> the Lord.
>
> —ACTS 3:19

The word *repent* means "to turn from, to turn around from one direction into another." In other words, the heart that turns completely to God receives renewal from the glorious presence of God.

Not all spiritual experiences lead us to renewal. In camps, crusades, or conferences, when confronted with certain truths, I used to feel remorse for my offenses and irresponsibility. That remorse would barely last a few hours or a few days. It was a repentance that led only to the altar, with tears, guilt, and frustration. This type of repentance does not lead us to a change or to renewal, however.

Acts 13:22 says that God chose David as king of Israel simply because he was a man after God's own heart. The believer who goes through an experience of renewal seeks to have a heart like the heart of God. In what way did David differ from so many others? He was different because the deepest desire of his heart was to know God. Read how he expressed his feelings:

> O God, you are my God, earnestly I seek you; my soul thirsts for you, my body longs for you, in a dry and weary land where there is no water. I have seen you in the sanctuary and beheld your power and your glory.
>
> —PSALM 63:1–2

Do you know what the fundamental difference was between King David and his son Solomon? Solomon was the wisest man in the world. When he realized that the responsibility for the kingdom was so great, he asked God for wisdom. He loved wisdom.

David had no thirst for wisdom, power, or victory. He hungered for God, for personal communion with his Creator. His soul was hungry for the living God, for the experience of God—not just the acceptance of godly truths. His most fervent desire was to come before God to worship and to know Him intimately.

Psalm 51 clearly explains how desperate David was to maintain that communion with God. After desiring a married woman, committing adultery with her, and planning the death of her husband so he could keep her, David cries in repentance:

> Create in me a pure heart, O God, and renew a steadfast spirit within me. Do not cast me from your presence or take your Holy Spirit from me.
>
> —PSALM 51:10–11

91

The Manifest Presence of God

Notice that David wasn't worried about the punishment he was going to receive. Neither was he concerned for his kingdom. He was anxious only about the possibility of losing the glorious manifest presence of the Holy Spirit.

You may say, "God is omnipresent. I can't lose His presence." Yes, the Bible teaches that we will never be able to get away from the presence of God. But read this Bible verse about the experience of Adam and Eve:

> Then the man and his wife heard the sound of the Lord God as he was walking in the garden in the cool of the day, and they hid from the Lord God among the trees of the garden.
>
> —Genesis 3:8

Even though they couldn't hide from the omnipresent presence of God, they ran away from the manifest presence of God.

> So Cain went out from the Lord's presence and lived in the land of Nod [this word means "wondering"], east of Eden.
>
> —Genesis 4:16

Even though Cain didn't run away from the omnipresent presence of God, he left the manifest glorious presence of the Creator.

> Say to them: "For the generations to come, if any of your descendants is ceremonially unclean and yet comes near the sacred offerings that the Israelites consecrate to the Lord, that person must be cut off from my presence. I am the Lord."
>
> —Leviticus 22:3

The children of Israel couldn't leave God's presence, but they could be cut off from the manifest glorious presence of God in the camp.

Yes, God is omnipresent. However, the Bible teaches us that His glory, His manifest presence, is not in every place and is not for everybody. The Bible also teaches us that we have to desire and to seek His manifest presence. How many times had I been in places, in churches, in crusades where the manifest presence of God could be felt? However, in my personal life there wasn't a search, a discipline, and a thirst for experiencing it every day. I did not particularly desire to be in the manifest presence of God.

Intellectually I was trying to justify myself for the daily absence of the manifestation of the presence of God in my life. I believed and preached that we didn't have to look for experiences, because the presence of God was omnipresent. However, this explanation was an excuse, a way of escaping the truth: I didn't know the manifest, personalized presence of the Holy Spirit in my own life. I was looking for the benefits of the manifestation of the presence of God—the gifts, the blessings, the anointing, the knowledge, and the authority—but I wasn't searching for the intimacy of the glorious manifest presence of God. That night in Toronto, I saw a man who sought and found the manifest presence of God, and together with thousands of others we were touched and transformed. I deeply repented. From that day on, I decided to seek God and His manifest presence as the central and most important thing in my life.

To have a repentant heart, totally directed unto God, is to do all that God wants. He does not want us to compromise with the natural mind and its thoughts. He does not want us to allow human nature to take over the work and the interests of God, governing and manipulating them.

This precisely has been our greatest downfall. Taking God's place has paralyzed us and prevented renewal. We have put ourselves in charge of the reformation and sanctification. We believe that we have to change ourselves—that we have to make every effort to manage to be like Jesus Christ.

Maybe in this attitude, there is something of Diotrephes' problem. The apostle John wrote: "But Diotrephes, who loves to be first, will have nothing to do with us" (3 John 9). Such an attitude doesn't yield to the cross of Jesus Christ; such a mind doesn't submit to the spirit of grace. Such people hold themselves in high esteem. This is very common among the people of God. However, if we want to be renewed, whatever wants to take first place in our life has to disappear. It is only then that Christ can work in us.

The Way to Worship

THE WORSHIPER IS A person who has directed his or her heart to God to do His will entirely. How does one start? With repentance.

The heart that leaves all human efforts and turns to God is ready to worship. But what constitutes worship to many in the Christian world?

To many, worship is a way of unloading the worries of one's life. In this case, the purpose of worship is to feel a relief from daily pressures. With this attitude, the soul focuses on the problems and burdens, not on God. The heart is not directed toward God but to one's own needs.

To others, worship is a way of rejoicing. To such, the purpose of worship is forgetting about difficult circumstances and experiencing happiness, joy, and tranquility. With this attitude, the soul focuses on itself, not on God.

Worship is also a way to relieve a sense of responsibility before God. After all, God is worthy of our worship. We have to worship Him—it is our duty. With this attitude, the soul is concerned with pleasing God and is carrying out its duty out of a fear of punishment. In church services, worship is just part of the program. But in the private devotional life, worship is not very important.

For the majority of believers, the most important thing

about worship is the prayer of supplication by which we present our needs to God. After all, God is the only one capable of supplying them. If we have a devotional life, we use it to present our list of needs, concerns, and worries to God. Worship is seemingly not important. Our hearts are not directed to God but to our own needs. Our heart has not turned to God, but to our human efforts to please God and to see if He will grant us our petitions. Our heart is directed inward, always contemplating our defective human condition.

That was me. I sacrificed myself to pray. It seemed to me that the more I prayed, the more I was pleasing God, and therefore, the faster He would answer. The approach to my relationship with God could be seen in the substance of my prayers.

My prayer for my life: Lord, help me. Lord, strengthen me. Lord, open the door. Lord, bless me. Lord, change me.

My prayer for my ministry: Lord, prosper. Lord, direct me. Lord, work in this situation. Lord, give me grace. Lord, use me.

My prayer for the work of God: Lord, remove this problem. Lord, solve that conflict. Lord, change this, now!

What is the problem with such praying? My heartbeat, the purpose of my life, the target of my vision, and the sense of my existence were totally directed inward; they were inverted. My being was constantly contemplating itself.

Our worship to God today is often directed by our life's needs. We have made God in our own image. In the cultures where prosperity and comfort are greatly emphasized, the God who provides is worshiped. In cultures where there is suffering because of injustice, God is the protector, the one who suffers with the poor.

When those who don't know Christ contemplate themselves, they arrive at the conclusion that they have to solve their inner conflicts with the things of this earth. For many, the prime goals are entertainment, accumulation of goods, power, alcohol, and drugs. People use such things to placate the emptiness of their inner lives.

When those who know Christ examine themselves, they conclude they have to solve their inner conflicts by pleasing God with religious activities and good moral behavior.

What is the main problem? Our hearts are directed toward ourselves, toward our thoughts. I don't have to explain to you what you already know about yourself. I don't have to explain to you what you feel inside when the lights go out and you lay your head on the pillow. Where do your thoughts go when the radio and the television are turned off, when the service and the music are over, when it is just you and your circumstances?

The current religious and philosophical trends in this world recommend other approaches. New Age, for example, teaches that we are gods. In order to reach peace and balance and develop to the fullness of our potential, we must focus inward, toward our soul, toward the "god" that we are. We can learn to do this by learning to meditate. The material world is harmful and bad. The good, the divine, is inside of us.

Materialism, on the other hand, teaches that peace and prosperity are achieved by accumulating goods, power, and influence. Its total focus is external.

New Age tells people to look inside to find peace and balance; materialism proclaims that well being can be found through the acquisition of goods and status. One looks inward—the other outward.

But where does the Bible exhort us to look? In chapter 12 of the Book of Hebrews we read: "We are surrounded by such a great cloud of witnesses . . . " (v. 1). These *witnesses* are men and women who have given us examples of faith. In spite of the impossibilities, they looked to Him who had promised them the victory.

We need to "throw off everything that hinders and the sin that so easily entangles. . . . " Can we, on our own, eliminate sin from our lives? No, a thousand times, no!

We have to "run with perseverance the race marked out

for us." Can we run with our own strength? No, a thousand times, no!

So, what should we do? Verses 2 and 3 of this same chapter say clearly, "Let us fix our eyes on Jesus, the author and perfecter of our faith, who for the joy set before him endured the cross, scorning its shame, and sat down at the right hand of the throne of God. Consider him who endured such opposition from sinful men, so that you will not grow weary and lose heart."

Which way should the believer focus his eyes? Toward Jesus Christ, the author and perfecter of the faith. He is the author of my faith. He is the generator of the faith in my life. I don't generate faith. I can pray, fast, and sacrifice to an extreme, yet none of these efforts will produce faith in my life. Faith is the only thing that pleases God. However, the kind of faith that pleases God is the faith that comes from Him. If we please God with faith, it is because He has made us suitable to please Him.

> May the God of peace, who through the blood of the
> eternal covenant brought back from the dead our Lord
> Jesus, that great Shepherd of the sheep, equip you with
> everything good for doing his will, and may he work in
> us what is pleasing to him, through Jesus Christ, to
> whom be glory for ever and ever. Amen.
> —HEBREWS 13:20–21

OUR EYES FIXED ON JESUS

NOWADAYS, A LOT of emphasis is placed on worship and praise. There are many worship recordings produced. In addition, worship and praise services are more and more common. However, I still wonder if we understand what real worship is all about. I have noticed three reactions to this current emphasis.

There is a group that is opposed to all the external movement of praise and worship. These people are concerned about the music, the musicians, and the external style. They are upset that the music is not adapted to their particular culture; they are insistent that there be no dance, and they are uneasy about the time spent in singing.

They talk about "types of worship"—acceptable and unacceptable worship—according to their particular denomination and its historical doctrines. Finally, they judge the motivations of those who lead this movement.

There is another group that is delighted. They buy all the recordings, attend all the concerts, and follow the men and women God has raised up to increase people's understanding of praise and worship. These are the ones sincerely interested in changing *all* the music, throwing away the "old and old-fashioned." They think that worship and praise groups, music and instruments, and books and teachings will enable us to reach a higher level of spirituality. Those who belong to this group have turned this movement into a crusade and a revolution. Yet, in spite of their good intentions, their whole commitment to praise and worship rests in the music, in concert after concert, conference after conference, and recording after recording.

However, there is a third group. *These are the true worshipers, those who don't worry about the music even though it is one of the most important elements of worship.* Their main goal is to have a heart like God's heart. Their eyes are fixed on God, on His promises, on the manifestation of God's glory in the nations, on His greatness, on the cross of Calvary, on the finished work of Christ, on the empty tomb, on the total and absolute victory against all principality and power, and on that Lamb who is seated at the throne, the author and perfecter of our faith. Their minds are on God's thoughts.

A true worshiper is aware of the truth, of God's thoughts. The truth is that we are sinners, filthy and imperfect, and the best we can offer God is nothing more than "filthy rags." But the truth also is that Christ came to take our place, to live a perfect life as our representative. He fulfilled the law of God that no one else could. Christ offered Himself willingly as an innocent sacrifice. He paid, settled, and eliminated the debt we had with God through His holy blood. During the last seconds of His life, on the cross at Calvary, He proclaimed that His work on my behalf was complete and finished. He exclaimed, "It is finished."

Now, the truth tells me that although I'm not just, I'm justified and declared innocent of all guilt because God favors me with His Son's justice. How do we obtain Christ's cloak of justice? How do we achieve justification for our sins? How do we find peace with God? Paul gives us the answer:

> Therefore, since we have been justified through faith, we have peace with God through our Lord Jesus Christ, through whom we have gained access by faith into this grace in which we now stand. And we rejoice in the hope of the glory of God.
>
> —ROMANS 5:1–2

In the Old Testament in Numbers 21, we read about the tragedy that took place in Israel. The Israelites were on their way to the Promised Land. The only thing God required of them was faith. But Israel, instead of believing in God, focused on the impossibilities, on the enemies they encountered in the desert.

On the path of faith, many obstacles will come our way to make us take our eyes away from the promise; many burdens and sins will present themselves and will cause us to stumble in the race. To arrive at the Promised Land of Canaan, Israel had to go through Edom. The Edomites descended from Esau and the Israelites from Jacob. They had the same blood lineage, but not the same spiritual lineage. Israel was from the lineage of Jacob, a man who desired God's blessing with all his heart. Edom was from the lineage of Esau, a man who had rejected the blessing of God.

The Edomites hated the Israelites, treating the Israelites

cruelly. They didn't allow Israel, with more than two million men, women, and children, to go through their territory. Israel had to choose a much longer route toward the Promised Land.

Because of this, the Israelites became discouraged. The people spoke against God and against Moses: "Why have you brought us up out of Egypt to die in the desert? There is no bread! There is no water! And we detest this miserable food!" (Num. 21:5).

The Israelites complained even though God was giving them manna every day, keeping them healthy, making sure their clothes and shoes didn't wear out, and protecting them constantly with a cloud by day and a pillar of fire by night. The situation with Edom caused them to turn their eyes toward the circumstances and blame God and Moses. Therefore, God answered. God always answers when we take our eyes away from Him. Numbers 21:6 records that "then the LORD sent venomous snakes among them; they bit the people and many Israelites died."

Suddenly, the Israelites forgot about the Edomites, the manna, the water, and all the inconveniences of the desert. Now the problem was the *serpents*.

God's discipline in our lives comes when we take our eyes away from Him and turn toward our need or to something or someone else. However, He doesn't discipline us to punish us, but to remind us that we need to fix our eyes on Jesus Christ, the author and perfecter of our faith.

The serpents produced a change in Israel. *They repented*.

> The people came to Moses and said, "We sinned when we spoke against the LORD and against you. Pray that the LORD will take the snakes away from us." So Moses prayed for the people. The LORD said to Moses, "Make a snake and put it up on a pole; anyone who is bitten can look at it and live."
>
> —NUMBERS 21:7–8

Read what Jesus said about this:

> Just as Moses lifted up the snake in the desert, so the
> Son of Man must be lifted up, that everyone who
> believes in him may have eternal life.
>
> —JOHN 3:14–15

To look at Christ means to believe in Him and in His
promises. To look at Christ means to adopt God's thoughts
as our thoughts. To fix our eyes on Jesus Christ is to believe
that He is the author of the faith in our lives. He is in charge
of our lives. He makes us right, directs us, and changes us.
Christ is the fountain of all blessing. In Him is all we need.
If our spiritual life or our behavior is failing because it's
missing something, He completes what is lacking.

GOD'S PURIFYING FIRE

ISAIAH RECEIVED THE marvelous revelation of worship in front
of the throne of God in the most critical moment of his life
(Isa. 6). King Uzziah, one of the kings most loved and
respected in the history of Israel because of the peace and
prosperity he had brought to the nation, was dying of lep-
rosy. According to the Law, lepers could not live among the
people. The throne, then, was empty. But God showed
Isaiah a throne that is never vacant. Even when the situation
is irreparable, there is a King and Lord seated permanently
on the throne. That throne is high and exalted.

The word *high* here means "lifted up." God revealed to
Isaiah a throne that was getting higher and higher. The
beautiful thing is that Isaiah was being lifted up with the
throne. Yet the authority, the power, and the majesty of
God are not simply big. God is constantly being exalted.
God gets higher and more exalted, without any limits and
without end.

Isaiah saw God in His holiness. The angels cover their
faces when they're in front of the holiness of God. They

can't contemplate God or His holiness, because he who does so is transformed. (See 2 Corinthians 3:18.) Angels are not created in the image of God and will never be transformed into the image of Christ by the Spirit of the Lord. That is for the redeemed. That was for Isaiah. Isaiah looked at God's holiness openly. He saw the whole place filled with the glory of God. But suddenly, Isaiah changed. He looked at himself and said:

> Woe to me! . . . I am ruined! For I am a man of unclean lips, and I live among a people of unclean lips, and my eyes have seen the King, the LORD Almighty.
>
> —ISAIAH 6:5

If we gaze at the holiness of God and then look at our own unclean condition, we will let out the same cry: "Woe to me, I am ruined!" Just to think that we need to please a perfect and holy God is enough to make us feel anxious. If you look for the word "woe" in the Bible, you will always find it in a context of judgments, punishments, and curses. When Isaiah stared at the holiness of God, he judged himself and spoke out the words: "I'm ruined."

But thank God, in heaven there is more than just His throne of holiness and judgment. There is another place that God showed Isaiah: an altar with a burning fire. The word *altar* means "place of sacrifice, place of death." It was a place of bloody sacrifice. On the altar of God there is blood, the blood of the Lamb. There is purification of sins by the blood of Jesus. When we confess with true repentance, repentance that is more than remorse and pain over our filthiness, we achieve justification by faith based on the consummate work of Christ on the cross.

Isaiah confessed. When we confess our sin, the Bible says:

> But if we walk in the light, as he is in the light, we have fellowship with one another, and the blood of

Jesus, his Son, purifies us from all sin....If we confess our sins, he is faithful and just and will forgive us our sins and purify us from all unrighteousness.

—1 JOHN 1:7–9

At the precise moment Isaiah confessed, God touched his unclean lips to purify them and declared:

See, this has touched your lips; your guilt is taken away and your sin atoned for.

—ISAIAH 6:7

God purified Isaiah after his confession in two aspects: *"Your guilt is taken away." Taken away* means "removed, dislodged, extracted, and transferred." *Guilt* means "depravity, twisted, and corrupted behavior." When God removes something, He removes it perfectly and completely. God removes our sins, our depraved behavior, our offenses, and our failures from our hearts. He takes them away and deposits them in total oblivion. He doesn't leave any guilt. We are declared innocent, as if we had never committed any sins.

"Your sin is atoned for." The word *atoned* means "covered." *Sin* means "sinful condition." When we confess, God forgives our sin, but He does not remove our sinful condition. The blood of Christ covers our condition of sinful and Adam-like nature. We will be transformed one day. Our corruptible body, our sinful flesh, and our Adam-like nature will be changed into a new glorified body. We will be like Him. In the meantime, the blood of Jesus Christ covers or hides our sinful nature because God can't look at sin.

We believe the sin that separates us from God is the daily sins, failures, falls, and offenses. Those sins are removed when we confess them. What truly separates us from God is our sinful nature, which was inherited from Adam. That condition cannot be eliminated. The only solution is to cover it.

During Passover, when God saw the blood over the doorframes of the Israelites, He "passed over" and didn't bring death into those houses. When He sees the blood of Christ over our depraved nature, He "passes over" our lives and accepts us in the Beloved.

Many will say, "How easy!" It is more demanding and difficult than it seems. This is the gospel of grace. These are God's thoughts. This is the way God perceives our lives. The one who understands and achieves grace also understands that he or she mustn't abuse grace. He who truly accepts grace doesn't abuse it, because he understands that Christ paid a very high price for us because of His love. We should be forever thankful.

My wife loves me deeply. She knows my imperfections, and yet, she loves me in spite of them. If I commit an offense, she forgives me. However, that assurance doesn't lead me to betray her. The security of her love makes me appreciate her more, protect her more, and love her more each day. The same thing happens with God. His love is unselfish. His grace is unmerited. The more I see the love and the grace of God, the more I'm revolted by sin.

Isaiah received God's forgiveness. His offenses were taken away and his sinful condition was covered. That produced an amazing thing. Suddenly, he started to hear a heavenly dialogue. As the blood was applied to his life, his ears were opened, and he could hear God saying, "Whom shall I send? And who will go for us?" (Isa. 6:8).

GOD'S CLOSENESS

GOD WASN'T TALKING to Isaiah. The members of the Trinity were conversing. They were looking for a messenger. God revealed His heart to Isaiah. After our purification, God always shows us the passion of His heart so that His will is announced to the people and His salvation declared.

Satan has spread a lie throughout history: He wants man to believe God is unreachable and so holy that He doesn't want to have communion with man. Nevertheless, the worshiper who knows the heart of God intimately doesn't believe the lie. God is our Father. He always takes the initiative. After Adam and Eve sinned, God didn't reject them. What happened was that "the man and his wife heard the sound of the LORD God as he was walking in the garden in the cool of the day, and they hid from the LORD God among the trees of the garden. But the LORD God called to the man, 'Where are you?'" (Gen. 3:8–9).

Since that day, God is always searching and asking, "Where are My children?" And man continues to run from God. Many times Christians avoid worshiping Him intimately. We like to sing, shout, dance, and talk. But when there is silence, many get nervous. When worship is discussed, many feel uncomfortable. We say that reflective hymns or slow songs are sad and depressing. We have believed the devil's lie that God is angry with us. He who begins to know God's heart in worship rapidly realizes God wants to communicate with His children. God wants to manifest His love, His grace, His forgiveness, and His warmth. He wants to bring all men to the altar to touch their lips, take away their guilt, and cleanse them from sin. God wants to take us to the fountain, which is Christ.

> On that day a fountain will be opened to the house of David and the inhabitants of Jerusalem, to cleanse them from sin and impurity.
> —ZECHARIAH 13:1

> He said to me: "It is done. I am the Alpha and the Omega, the Beginning and the End. To him who is thirsty I will give to drink without cost from the spring of the water of life. He who overcomes will inherit all this, and I will be his God and he will be my son."
> —REVELATION 21:6–7

God wants the gospel of Jesus Christ, the Good News, to

be announced. We have conceived an "exclusivist" God who only takes care of His children. We have conceived a God who only cares about the "perfect, mature, and holy." God is also interested in the rebellious, the disobedient, and the ones who have gone astray. There is still hope!

When I finally understood this truth, I was renewed. In my mind, I mark the difference between David before his renewal and David after he was renewed. He who learns to know the desire of God's heart is renewed. He who learns to know and believe in God's thoughts is transformed from glory to glory. The great thing about this is that the desire of God's heart has no limits and no end; it is eternal. We will forever be knowing and contemplating the desire of His heart. Would you like to know Jesus' heart's desire toward His church? Would you like to know Jesus' thoughts toward His bride?

John saw Jesus on the island of Patmos. In His message to the church in Laodicea, Jesus says:

> Here I am! I stand at the door and knock. If anyone hears my voice and opens the door, I will come in and eat with him, and he with me. To him who overcomes, I will give the right to sit with me on my throne, just as I overcame and sat down with my Father on his throne. He who has an ear, let him hear what the Spirit says to the churches.
>
> —REVELATION 3:20–22

Isaiah heard the voice of God. When he heard God's heart's desire, he answered: "Here am I. Send me!" (Isa. 6:8).

A WORSHIPING HEART

WHAT IS WORSHIP? When do we worship God? Is worship what takes place in the services or in our prayer closet? Does it mean to raise our hands, sing worship songs, cry, pray, bow down, and close our eyes? All these things can be part of worship.

Worshiping God is the heart's condition of those sons and daughters of God who live in an ongoing state of repentance, longing and seeking for God's manifest presence. It is the heart's condition of the Christian who accepts God's grace, which is the expression of His heart.

It is the heart that contemplates, believes, and surrenders to the Lord's will.

It is the Christian who gives time to God for Him to put His heart, His image, His interests, His purposes, and His thoughts into his or her heart.

If we combine music with lyrics from a worshiping heart, the music becomes a powerful force that helps us, encourages us, and motivates us to bow down before our King, Jesus Christ.

There are musicians who sing because they were born with great vocal, musical, and poetical talent. But there are musicians who sing because they have gone through the experience of Isaiah or that of John on the island of Patmos, bowing down before the feet of Jesus Christ and crucifying the ego. Their hearts long for God. Their longing flows through the music and lyrics of their songs. They project the heart of God and His thoughts.

We can define worship in five different ways.

1. Worship is a condition of the heart.

The condition of a worshiper's heart is one of ongoing repentance. Not just simple remorse because of some offense, but a change of direction of the heart toward God. The heart of the worshiper is not concerned with what the natural mind says, nor with the convenient or pragmatic, but it is totally focused on God's will and purposes.

2. Worship is accepting God's grace.

He who doesn't understand the New Covenant and the finished work of Christ on the cross can't be a true worshiper.

107

There can't be freedom or sure entrance to the throne of grace without revelation of the love of God, of the sacrifice of Christ on our behalf, and of justification by faith. There can't be true worship when one combines salvation by faith with salvation by works and human efforts. There can't be an open entrance to the throne without understanding the New Covenant in the blood of our Lord Jesus Christ. The worshiper lives in the New Covenant and understands what it is to be under the blood of the New Covenant and cleansed from all sin. The worshiper accepts the love of God and delights in his communion with the Father who accepts him unconditionally because Christ has made him worthy.

What a tragedy it is that a majority of Christians worship with wrong, erroneous ideas. How many still think today that God is a demanding and tough God? The simple truth is this: There is nothing we can do to please God. Christ pleased Him completely and eternally in our place. The work of Christ was so perfect that it satisfied the Father entirely and eternally. When God stares at me, He not only accepts me, but He also delights in me and sings with joy. We are the children who were lost, and now, in Jesus Christ, we have come back to communion with our Father. Our Father delights in us!

3. Worship is contemplating God's heart.

To the worshipers, God uncovers His heart, His will, and His thoughts. God reveals His heart only in the depth of intimacy in the secret place of worship. Worshipers know the heart of God. I have been exhorted by Christians that have used the Word of God as a punishing whip, thinking that they were expressing the heart of God. They knew the Word of God—but they didn't know the God of the Word. They did not know the heart of the Father. They were not worshipers. I often hear people talking about God, His character, and His purposes, but they don't seem to be talking about the same God who opens His heart in times of worship. Sometimes I feel like shouting at them: "That is not the God I know! Don't talk about my God that way!"

God's heart is love for His children. God's heart is a Father's heart. God's heart was manifested in the years Jesus lived on earth. His birth in a manger, His childhood and youth in anonymity, His submission to His earthly parents, His surrender to the will of the Father and the Holy Spirit by choosing not to use His divine powers, His patience and love for His weak disciples, and His total yielding to death on the cross are clear revelations of God's love for us. Christ came, suffered, and died just for us. That is the heart of the Father; that is the heart of God! The worshiper gazes at the love, the grace, and the patience of God, our Father.

4. Worship is surrendering to God's heart.

In the place of worship, as we gaze at God's heart, we say what Isaiah said: "Here am I." Who can resist this Father who is so loving that He seduces us with His grace? It is easy to surrender to this God! To *surrender* means "to stop fighting." We no longer fight with God. He is Lord, and we will act according to His heart and His will. As Christians, our worst enemy is not the devil. It is God. Let us never quarrel with Him, because He always wins and we always lose. As Isaiah 45:9 says:

> Woe to him who quarrels with his Maker, to him who is but a potsherd among the potsherds on the ground. Does the clay say to the potter, "What are you making?" Does your work say, "He has no hands"?

5. Worship is the transformation of our heart.

A worshiping heart is a transformed heart. The worshiper who contemplates God's loving heart is transformed. The worshiper knows he has been forgiven and covered. He knows the Lord is the one who makes us "suitable" to carry out His will. He makes us fit when He takes our selfish, sinful, interested, and shortsighted hearts and changes them. How does He do it? By exposing our hearts to His heart. By revealing His character to us, exposing us to His light, revealing His love to us. Each time a heart has a true encounter with the heart of God, it doesn't resist—it changes.

Our hearts are like the celluloid used in film for a camera. The film is wrapped in a sealed container that light cannot penetrate. When the film is placed inside the camera, it is in absolute darkness. However, when a photograph is taken, the lens opens and allows the light to enter, putting its impression upon the film.

Such is the presence of the Lord. When we are exposed to His heart and presence, He seals us and prints His image upon our hearts. That image is the image of the character, the anointing, and the victory of Jesus Christ the Son of God. God transforms us in such a way that we end up experiencing what John voiced:

> He must become greater; I must become less.
>
> —JOHN 3:30

Paul said:

> I have been crucified with Christ and I no longer live, but Christ lives in me. The life I live in the body, I live by faith in the Son of God, who loved me and gave himself for me.
>
> —GALATIANS 2:20

When we consistently experience this, we are renewed in His image until our heart loses its influence and the heart of Christ dominates in us, until our will ceases to submit to the thoughts of the mind and submits to the thoughts of God. That is the renewal of a worshiper.

Eight

IN COMMUNION WITH THE HEART OF GOD

THERE ARE TWO aspects of the Christian life that concern us very much: personal evangelization and prayer. From the pulpit, through the books we read, and in radio and television messages, we receive exhortations about our duty as Christians to testify and pray more. Christians need to evangelize the lost! Believers need to pray unceasingly! But the majority of Christians do not carry out these mandates, and therefore, they carry a great sense of guilt.

In these last two years, I've talked to hundreds of people about their prayer lives. And they all have confessed that:

- They don't have an effective prayer life.
- They would like to have a disciplined prayer life.
- They feel guilty, sensing a hindrance in their hearts that is preventing this desire from becoming a reality.

I totally identify with them. I also used to feel like that. Whenever I would hear testimonies of other Christians' victories and experiences in prayer, I would feel really bad. Why? Because in my heart there was a strong desire to experience the same thing, but it wasn't happening.

I have always tried to develop a disciplined prayer life. I have always loved to read books on prayer. But many of those books talked about the "price" one needs to pay in the practice of prayer—the physical sacrifices, the many hours one has to be in prayer in order to achieve an answer. The more I read, the more afraid I was, and the less I prayed.

When I started to work at Radio Vision, I discovered the leaders, volunteers, and programmers liked to pray. That made me happy, because I thought it would help me to be more consistent in prayer. And so it did. The influence of these prayerful brothers and sisters helped me to pray daily for the needs of that new, needy, and economically poor ministry. But I continued to feel guilty. I wasn't praying from my heart. I was praying because we needed God's help. I felt *obligated* to pray.

Do you pray because you need something from God? Do you pray because the Bible tells you to do so and because every Christian is supposed to do it? If these are your motivations, don't feel too bad. Millions of Christians around the world share these same motivations.

Several local pastors attended a conference where a very well-known pastor who had written a book about prayer was speaking. He spoke about his church's amazing growth. From a handful of people, it had grown to more than seven thousand members. He attributed that growth to prayer, not only in his personal life, but also in the life of the church. Every day at 5:00 A.M., his church would get together to pray.

My friends came back from that conference feeling highly motivated. Several decided to follow the example and open their churches every day at 5:00 A.M. to pray. The late Pastor Miguel Mena, vice president of the board of Radio Vision, suggested that we should broadcast a live morning prayer service, so we did. Pastor Pablo Fernández, also a board member, suggested that we produce a radio announcement calling radio listeners to pray at five o'clock sharp every morning.

This emphasis on morning prayer produced tremendous fruit in the lives of the people and churches involved. I myself felt motivated to get up to pray with them. Every night, I set my alarm clock to wake me up at the appointed time. I got up and prayed at home, along with my brothers who were praying at the church. My heart was burning. I had always liked to be committed to prayer, although I feared doing it only out of obligation. But one night, because of a ministry engagement, I arrived home very late. I couldn't get up at five the next morning. When I woke up, I felt terribly guilty.

From that day on, it became very hard for me to get up at five to pray. It was during those days that we were starting the negotiations to buy the radio station. We had to move, buy a new building, and remodel the offices and studios. I came home very tired each evening. I could no longer get up that early. Yet I knew if I did not get up at five, I would lose the opportunity to pray with the brothers through the radio.

It was discouraging, because I had always been looking for somebody with whom I could pray. When in a group, I could pray for a long time, but when I was alone, I found it very difficult to concentrate. My prayer life was a violent struggle, consisting mainly of one petition: "Lord, help me to be a man of prayer!" My constant prayer was about prayer. I was obsessed.

To the Difficult Through the Easy

So many who speak about prayer concentrate on the difficult and costly aspects of it. Often when we get ready to pray, we feel we must:

- Kneel
- Present specific petitions
- Pray with faith
- Pray unceasingly

- Feel the presence of God
- Hear the voice of God
- Obtain answers
- Suffer and agonize

Many of these concepts scared me. If the purpose of our preaching about prayer is to encourage others to pray, we should talk less about the cost of prayer and more about the benefits and delights of prayer.

God knows how to change us; He isn't interested in causing us pain or suffering. He treats us the way a good father treats his little child. When God started to renew me, He didn't start from the *prayer* side—He started from the *pleasant* side: the worship. I have always liked music and praise. However, I have always struggled with the discipline of prayer. God is my Father, and He has sent His Holy Spirit to carry out His program in me.

During those first days of renewal, I started to understand what true worship was all about. Worship is the constant state of a heart that gazes at the revelation of the heart of God.

In worship, God reveals His heart to us, compelling us to contemplate Him, admire Him, and humble ourselves in His presence, recognizing that although we aren't worthy, we are His children. Worship leads us to prayer. In worship, we contemplate; in prayer, we come into communion with the heart of God. In worship, we marvel. In prayer, we get closer; we touch the heart of God, and His heart touches ours.

The heart of God is His character, His will, His purposes, and His thoughts. In prayer, my spirit becomes one with the Spirit of God. My will becomes completely one with the will of God. My thoughts become one with God's thoughts. After gazing at God's heart through worship, a clamor rises in me: "God, I want to be like You! Lord, I want to have a heart in accordance with Yours! Lord, Your heart beats for lost souls. You are merciful and patient, slow to anger. You are willing to run to help me. I want to be like that! Change me!"

When we see God's heart and long for it, then we reach His heart.

David was a man after God's heart; he longed to be like Him. David's desire was to be pure and holy like God. However, David confessed: "Surely I was sinful at birth, sinful from the time my mother conceived me" (Ps. 51:5). That is why he declared: "Surely you desire truth in the inner parts; you teach me wisdom in the inmost place" (v. 6). In his times of worship, of intimacy with God in the secret place, David understood the wisdom of God. That is why he prayed: "Create in me a pure heart, O God, and renew a steadfast spirit within me" (v. 10).

God loves the true and honest heart. A humble heart, bowed down in adoration, asking to be renewed, moves the creative hand of God. The word *create* is a term used exclusively in reference to God. It is used eleven times in the Book of Genesis—in relationship to the creation of the heavens, the earth, the animals, the man, and the woman. It implies the formation of something that didn't exist before. Only God could have created the heavens and the earth out of nothing. Everything God created was in Him from before the foundation of time. When the perfect moment arrived, God pronounced the creative word, and everything came into being.

God also creates a clean heart in me; when it withers, He renews it and returns it to its original condition of purity. That victorious and vibrant renewed heart exists in the heart of God. When we long for it, when we confess our poverty of spirit, God pronounces a word and creates in us a renewed heart according to His own heart, making us participants of His divine nature. In the same way that God created the world by simply speaking a word, He also creates a new heart by speaking His thoughts to our heart.

If there is anything that pleases the heart of God, it is a heart that acknowledges its offenses, humbles itself before the God of all grace, claims sonship, contemplates the revelation of divine love, and longs to be transformed.

In worship, God shows me His loving heart. He reveals to me His will, His master plan, and His grace.

In prayer, God reveals to me His will and His desire for every moment of my life. God wants us to know His will for every situation. He does this because He knows our needs, our weaknesses, our past, our present, and our future. He knows we can't survive without the knowledge of His will. That is why in worship, before anything else, He reveals to us His will as a whole and His Father's heart.

When we receive the revelation of God's heart for that specific moment, something wonderful happens. Faith is born. What is faith?

> Now faith is being sure of what we hope for and certain of what we do not see.
> —HEBREWS 11:1

In prayer, God reveals to us His position regarding the circumstances that He wants us to know. When we discern God's heart, we realize He is already at work. Everything is under His control. When we know He is participating in the matter, faith is born. When God is in charge of something, the only thing that remains to do is to be thankful, receive it, and keep on waiting on Him.

For quite a while there have been some hindrances to our radio ministry that human decisions, money, or technical resources can't solve. They are barriers of pride and distrust—erected by people who are obstructing the will of God. I have tried to solve this problem; I have prayed, begged, and interceded with God to set us free, but my prayer hasn't been answered. God hasn't removed those obstacles yet.

Recently while praying, God showed me His will. In His heart, those problems were already solved. When I realized He had already intervened in the situation, faith was born in my heart, and I believed. The reality is that I haven't seen the fulfillment yet; the obstacles still remain, but they don't bother me anymore. When I look at the problems, I give thanks to God because I know He is already removing them. I have faith. My faith didn't come because I heard an inspiring message. My faith came from the Word of God and the preaching of the Word.

When we have communion with God, we share our being with Him, and He shares His being with us. This is an uneven exchange. A believer brings his or her weak and anxious being and presents it as an offering to God; God accepts the offering and shares His nature with the believer. God, through His Holy Spirit, imparts His comfort, power, love, grace, direction, wisdom, and all spiritual blessing in the heavenly places to us. In communion, there is an exchange of lives. I give Him my life, and He gives me His.

As God shares His greatness, His very life with me, my answer to God is faith. I don't produce faith. I don't have to manipulate my emotions to be able to feel faith. I don't have to enter into a psychological frenzy to be able to feel enthusiasm, optimism, and hope. Faith is a gift of God. Faith is a gift God gives to worshipers who share with Him in communion.

- Without communion, there is no faith.
- Without true prayer, there is no faith.
- Without worship, there is no faith.
- Without the revelation of the heart of God, there is no faith.
- Faith is my response to such revelation.

That is why faith comes from hearing the Word of God. In Romans 10:17, the apostle Paul says that faith comes by hearing the *rhema* of God. The word *rhema* means "enlightened word, chosen for a specific purpose." Have you ever read a familiar passage in the Bible and suddenly found the answer to a difficult situation you were going through at that very moment? Have you ever read a familiar passage that suddenly had a profound impact on you, as if you had read it for the first time? The Holy Spirit enlightened that passage, that verse, so that the will of God would be revealed to you in that moment.

This verse teaches us that the revelation of God's heart, the manifestation of His will and His purpose during times of communion, produces faith.

Why Don't We Pray?

We don't pray because we don't understand what prayer is. Many people believe prayer is a spiritual exercise that demands suffering and is very costly. Others don't pray because they don't know the Father. They have the concept of a terrifying God. When people ask me what God I believe in, I respond that I believe in God, the Father of our Lord Jesus Christ. Jesus Christ came to reveal God the Father to us. The Pharisees were shocked when they heard Jesus call the Father *abba,* which can be translated as "daddy." Jesus didn't call Him *Lord of hosts*—He called Him "Dad." Jesus taught us to pray to the "Father who is in heaven."

Others don't pray because they haven't received answers to their prayers in the past. Perhaps you've presented your petitions to the Lord with all the sincerity of your soul, but apparently, God didn't hear your prayer because He didn't answer.

When God Remains Silent

When God doesn't seem to be answering our prayers, it may be because our prayers are incorrect. Or our prayers may cover so many things that we don't grasp all they represent, so God takes time to answer them. The will of God isn't just a way to find an answer to our prayers; it is the way by which we learn to discern His heart.

Prayer is not a tool to use to obtain something from God. Prayer is our means for having perfect communion with Him. Prayer enables us to become one with God. We are not God's clients. In prayer, we don't go to Him to buy something that is paid with sacrifice, with insistence, and with devotion. We are His children. He is our Father. He doesn't listen to us because of our devotion; He listens because we are His children, redeemed by the blood of Jesus Christ.

If we come to the place of prayer just to ask, we are like the capricious bride who presented a list of conditions for marriage to her groom. She was only willing to marry him if he committed to supply her with a comfortable home, money, a good car, financial security for the rest of her life, much happiness, and complete health. Many believers approach the Lord in prayer with a shopping list in hand. "Lord, give me this . . . and that . . . and also that. . . . If You give me this . . . I will feel good, I will pray more, and I will serve You." Let's get the correct idea:

- We don't pray to feel the presence of God, although we do feel it.
- We don't pray to receive an answer from Him, although we will receive one.
- We don't pray to receive spiritual experiences, although they will happen.
- We don't pray to receive peace, although it will come.
- We don't pray to explain our problems to Him, although we will explain them.

We pray to be one with God so He will show us His will. We don't pray just to tell Him in detail our pains and our struggles, but rather for Him to explain to us His will in the midst of our pains and our struggles. We pray so that He shows us His will in the face of our daily temptations.

"Delight yourself also in the LORD, and He shall give you the desires of your heart," (Ps. 37:4, NKJV). My understanding of this verse used to be the following: If I delight myself in the Lord, all the desires hidden in my heart will be granted. God will delight so much in me that He will give me whatever I ask Him. No! That is not what this verse says.

The word *delight* means "to be malleable, soft, and flexible." The psalmist is exhorting us to be willing to be molded by God. If I allow God to mold me, the psalm goes on to say that God will give me something. The word *give* conveys the idea of "producing." In the life that is being molded, God produces fruit.

God promises to grant "the desires of your heart." In the life that already has been molded, God produces the fruit of certain desires. Those desires are produced by God and are according to His will. The word *desire* also implies a petition or a request. If we delight ourselves in the Lord, He will produce petitions in our hearts.

Our requests are selfish, human, and shortsighted. The petitions of our High Priest, who constantly intercedes for us, are perfect and according to the will of the Father. The person who allows God to mold him will have divine desires, heavenly requests, and prayers that reflect the will and desire of God.

One morning, as I was worshiping the Lord during the radio program, I felt a strong impulse from the Holy Spirit, a voice that clearly told me, "Ask now!"

I took my wallet out, put it on the transmission table, and said, "Lord, right now You are telling me to ask. You are putting this petition inside of me; I had no plans to do it. Lord, here are my financial needs. Provide for us. Thank You. Amen."

For a long time I had been praying for our needs! Many times, it had seemed to me that the more I asked, the sadder and more worried I remained. But there is a big difference when God places in our hearts the petition to pray for something specifically. In that moment, God revealed to me His will, His heart, in regards to a particular circumstance. Having revealed His will to me, He placed His request in me and gave me faith to ask. What is done in God's heart will be done on earth. When God places a heavenly petition in my heart, it is because it will be done on earth. I'm not ashamed to tell you that I am still waiting for all my financial needs to be solved. However, there is one thing I know with absolute faith. God put in me His request. His petition was placed in my heart. He produced the faith in me to ask for something that had been done already in the heavens, in His will. The Word tells me that if I ask according to His will, His heart, and His desires, whatever I ask in His name "is done."

> This is the confidence we have in approaching God: that if we ask anything according to his will, he hears us. And if we know that he hears us—whatever we ask—we know that we have what we asked of him.
> —1 JOHN 5:14–15

"TEACH US TO PRAY"

IN LUKE 11:1, THE disciples asked Jesus, "Lord, teach us to pray, just as John taught his disciples." How did John pray? What had he taught about prayer? John the Baptist was an Old Covenant prophet, subject to the Law of Moses. As a good Jew, he prayed three times a day, repeating automatically the Hebrew prayers.

But Jesus answered, "When you pray, say..." (Luke 11:2). Jesus gave them a new revelation. In chapter 6 of Matthew, Jesus talks about two activities we are to do in secret: give to the needy and pray. He taught that the Father rewards these two activities when done in secret, according to the law of Christ. And to all this He added:

> For your Father knows what you need before you ask him.
> —MATTHEW 6:8

Jesus tells us to ask the Father. We understand that to ask

is to pray, to beg, to present a request based on a need. But the "asking" Jesus is talking about is that of a citizen who asks the protection of his government, or that of a child who asks to eat at his parents' table, or that of a person who complains about a purchased product or a service.

Do you remember the parable of the good Samaritan? After the wounded man was taken care of, the good Samaritan took him to a hotel and paid for his stay. Everything the man needed was provided, and the good Samaritan promised he would pay for any extra charges when he returned. The man didn't have to worry about his expenses because the Samaritan had already paid for them in advance! (See Luke 10:30–35.)

We can ask God for whatever we need because it is already ours; it is at our disposal. We don't have to beg or entreat to see if maybe God will feel sorry for us and answer. When we pray, we invoke "Our Father in heaven" as Jesus taught us (Matt. 6:9).

He is our Father, and we are His children. We didn't earn the privilege of being His children. Jesus obtained that beautiful privilege for us through His life, death, and Resurrection. That is why He teaches us God is our Father who is in the heavens.

God doesn't operate according to earth's limitations. He is in the heavens and is the absolute Lord of that place. Ephesians 1:3 says, "Praise be to the God and Father of our Lord Jesus Christ, who has blessed us in the heavenly realms with every spiritual blessing in Christ."

In the heavens, there are no limits, no obstacles. Notice carefully that our Father who is in heaven has "every spiritual blessing" at our disposal. Where are these blessings? In the heavenly places, in the heavens, in Christ. Our Father is the only one who can bless us. He is the only one for whom we have to search. To Him alone should we pray. To Him alone should we make our requests. What do we ask for then, knowing it has been already provided? Jesus suggested asking for three things:

In Communion With the Heart of God

1. "Hallowed be your name" (Matt. 6:9).

God's name has to be hallowed in our life. How do we hallow or sanctify the name of God? He is sanctified when we honor His holy and worthy name in our lives, in our families, in our work, in our plans, in our behavior, in our secret thoughts, and in private. God is honored when every aspect of our lives reflects His purity and His holiness. That is why, after worshiping our holy Father in the heavens, we want to be like Him. The first cry of the heart that is gazing at the Father is: "All that I have, all that I am, has to be purified, has to be changed into Your likeness, according to Your will."

2. "Your kingdom come" (Matt. 6:10).

The Word of God says:

> But if I drive out demons by the Spirit of God, then the kingdom of God has come upon you.
> —MATTHEW 12:28

> When Jesus had called the Twelve together, he gave them power and authority to drive out all demons and to cure diseases, and he sent them out to preach the kingdom of God and to heal the sick.
> —LUKE 9:1–2

> For the kingdom of God is not a matter of eating and drinking, but of righteousness, peace and joy in the Holy Spirit.
> —ROMANS 14:17

> For the kingdom of God is not a matter of talk but of power.
> —1 CORINTHIANS 4:20

> Nor will people say, "Here it is," or "There it is," because the kingdom of God is within you.
>
> —LUKE 17:21

The kingdom of God comes upon me when the Holy Spirit imparts the justice of Christ to me by grace, when He gives me peace and joy, and when He manifests His gifts of power, healing, and deliverance. The kingdom of God comes upon my life when all demonic power is bound and cast out. It comes when the power of God is manifested by pulling down demonic and carnal strongholds. The kingdom of God comes when Jesus Christ shows that He is the same yesterday, today, and forever.

After realizing the Father wants to give us all spiritual blessing in the heavenly realms, our hearts respond:

> *Lord, may everything in my life honor You. Lord, may all that I am and all that I have dignify Your holy and glorious name. Lord, there are things in my life that don't bring You honor. May Your kingdom of power, health, and authority come over everything that doesn't honor You and sanctify Your name.*

3. *"Your will be done on earth as it is in heaven"* (Matt. 6:10).

Herein lies the secret: Whatever we see in the heart of God, in the heart of our Father in heaven, is done. Whatever takes place in the heavenly heart of the Father is realized and accomplished. In the kingdom of God, everything happens in the heavens first and then is manifested on earth. Here is the true meaning of prayer: In prayer, the believer discerns the heart of God, and he makes sure that in God's time it will be visibly manifested.

I repeat, that is why we do not pray simply so that God will "move" or so that our petitions may be granted. God

124

can answer our prayers without concrete results that we can see. In prayer, we receive the answer by *faith*. There is no other option. We know God has answered our prayer because we have seen and discerned His heart. There is a big difference between simply believing "just because" and a belief that arises as the result of communion with the heart of God, where we have already seen the answer.

When we enter into a more personal relationship with the heart of God, we realize that He is concerned with three basic human needs:

1. *Our daily bread*

From first grade until I graduated from the university, my parents were in charge of my education and my well-being; they taught me how to properly behave in the context of our family and our society. One of the most important lessons they taught me was to respect others. They also taught me to fear them and to expect discipline if I disobeyed their wishes. Good parents want their children to be healthy, to have a career that will allow them to face life's challenges, and to have the ability to live in society, develop friendships, and be accepted. If my earthly father took such good care of me, and if my mother gave me such good and healthy nutrition, how much more will our heavenly Father give us.

Notice carefully that Jesus doesn't tell us to ask for bread. He simply tells us to declare before the Father that the daily bread comes from Him. When we present our requests to the Father, we don't beg as orphans do. We know that in His will we will have bread until the very last day of our lives on earth. We do not worry about tomorrow's bread because it has been already provided. In the prayer from child to Father, we simply express confidence, patience, and faith in our provider. We don't receive bread because of our sacrifice, devotion, or the hours we spend in His presence. We receive it because He is our Father.

2. *The forgiveness of our sins*

The same happens with the forgiveness of our sins. The Lord didn't tell us to ask to be forgiven. Jesus knew our sins were going to be paid for on the cross. Because our debt has been already paid, we don't have to ask for it to be paid again. Supplications, sacrifices, and penance do not produce forgiveness. We simply confess our sins, and He cleanses us from all our past, present, and future sins. In this prayer, we appropriate the forgiveness that God has already granted to us in His heart.

3. *Protection from the temptations and evil that surround us*

It is the same with temptations. Jesus tells us to expect our Father not to lead us into any temptation. This is neither a petition nor a request. Our Father never leads us toward evil. Satan does, but not our Father. God has prepared paths of goodness, blessing, and grace for us.

I once heard a story of a poor Texas farmer. He lived a life full of sacrifices. He worked the land until very late in life. Never able to succeed economically, he lived all his life in a hut with no running water, no electricity, and no comfort.

Before he died, a very rich executive visited him. This executive informed the farmer that although he had always been very poor, he was actually very rich. The land that had never rewarded him with the fruit of his labors was a gigantic oil deposit. The farmer was a millionaire, and he didn't know it. Right under his feet lay a huge oil treasure. He had never been poor—he was rich, but he didn't know it.

THE HIDDEN PURPOSES OF GOD

JESUS ENDS His prayer with praise:

For thine is the kingdom, and the power, and the glory, for ever. Amen.

—MATTHEW 6:13, KJV

Every prayer needs to end in praise. The believer who has contemplated the heart of the Father, discerned His purposes, and by faith appropriated spiritual blessings according to the Father's heart will end up rejoicing. The reason for our joy, even though we still haven't received the manifestation of the blessing, is based upon the fact that our Father is the owner of the kingdom, and He possesses unlimited power and glory forever.

Alleluia!

So then, how should we pray? Knowing our bread, forgiveness, and protection are secure, we need to pray, not begging, but knowing in the heart of our Father who is in heaven there are spiritual and material blessings that have been provided and paid for already.

When we commune with our Father, He reveals His desires and purposes for our lives to us, purposes that are hidden in His heart. And when God reveals them to us, we are renewed. The same thing that happened to the apostle Peter will happen to us:

When Jesus came to the region of Caesarea Philippi, he asked his disciples, "Who do people say the Son of Man is?"

They replied, "Some say John the Baptist; others say Elijah; and still others, Jeremiah or one of the prophets."

"But what about you?" he asked. "Who do you say I am?"

Simon Peter answered, "You are the Christ, the Son of the living God."

Jesus replied, "Blessed are you, Simon son of Jonah, for this was not revealed to you by man, but by my Father in heaven. And I tell you that you are Peter...."

—MATTHEW 16:13–18

127

Simon, son of Jonah, wanted to know the Messiah. He was a determined and violent man. He had been a member of a group called the Zealots. However, when the Father revealed His heart to him, Simon saw Jesus, the Christ. When he received this revelation, his life changed. From being *Simon*, the Jewish Zealot, he became *Peter*, the little rock. When the Father reveals His heart and His purposes to us, we change—He changes us. Then we have no more doubts, no more hesitations. We are sure because we know the will of the Father.

Moments With God

It is necessary for us to develop a prayer life and dedicate time to the Lord. The most important element we offer Him in prayer is time. Have you ever seen how the foundations of a house are laid? First, measurements are taken. Stakes are placed in the ground that will determine the size of the foundations. Then the ground is excavated and filled with cement. The deeper the excavation, the more cement that will be needed. The more cement, the stronger the foundation.

In prayer, we dig to build the foundations so God can come and fill us with His revelation. The foundations are made of time—minutes and hours that we give to our Father so He can bring revelation and transformation to our lives. The less time we spend with Him, the less revelation we will receive.

What do we do once we have separated the necessary time to pray and have communion with the Father? We worship. We contemplate. We sing. We humble ourselves. We wait. Then, we wait some more. We do not remain passive, but we worship, sing, raise our hands, and confess our offenses and our longing to be like Jesus. During the periods of waiting, the Holy Spirit intervenes.

The Holy Spirit brings us life in those times of waiting. The Bible asserts this:

Then we will not turn away from you; revive us, and we will call on your name. Restore us, O LORD God Almighty; make your face shine upon us, that we may be saved.

—PSALM 80:18–19

For this is what the high and lofty One says—he who lives forever, whose name is holy: "I live in a high and holy place, but also with him who is contrite and lowly in spirit, to revive the spirit of the lowly and to revive the heart of the contrite."

—ISAIAH 57:15

And if the Spirit of him who raised Jesus from the dead is living in you, he who raised Christ from the dead will also give life to your mortal bodies through his Spirit, who lives in you.

—ROMANS 8:11

In those times when all we can do is declare our brokenness, our incompetence before the Father, the Holy Spirit blows a gust of living wind over us.

In the same way, the Spirit helps us in our weakness. We do not know what we ought to pray for, but the Spirit himself intercedes for us with groans that words cannot express. And he who searches our hearts knows the mind of the Spirit, because the Spirit intercedes for the saints in accordance with God's will. And we know that in all things God works for the good of those who love him, who have been called according to his purpose.

—ROMANS 8:26–28

The Bible teaches that Jesus is our High Priest. He is our intercessor. He is constantly interceding for us. And the wonderful thing is that He is the only one who knows exactly what to pray for us, because He knows what we truly need. I don't know what He's praying to the Father on my behalf, but the Holy Spirit knows. When He revives us, the Holy Spirit reveals to us the intercessory prayer of Christ and the enlightened word for that precise moment and situation.

Jesus said, "It is written: 'Man does not live on bread alone, but on every word that comes from the mouth of God'" (Matt. 4:4).

That word (*rhema*) is an enlightened word of life, revitalized for a specific moment or situation. To grasp it is not just simply to read the Bible. It is to know that a Bible passage is God's message for a determined situation in time. It is to know that Jesus is praying the exact same prayer in heaven.

The Holy Spirit reveals that to us. When He does, the prayer in the Spirit is born. We become one with the heart of Jesus, we have communion with the Father, we pray the same prayer our High Priest is praying, and our prayer finds an answer. The Father always grants His Son's petitions on our behalf.

So therefore, sing and worship the Lord until the Holy Spirit revives you. Wait. Often we talk so much when we pray that even though the Holy Spirit wants to revive us, He can't. Remember: The all-powerful prayer is the one that the Holy Spirit has inspired.

Prayer is all-powerful when the Holy Spirit reveals the intercessory prayer of Jesus on our behalf to us. Jesus is omnipotent.

When we haven't developed true communion with God in prayer, we are basically praying to ourselves. When there is no relationship, we pray out of need, because of the predicament we're in or just because we feel we have to. When there is no intimacy, one prays to relieve the guilt. When our heart is not one with God's heart, we pray to receive some blessing or to have an experience. The prayer is mechanical. There is no worship. We don't know the heart of God. We don't have the patience or the time to wait for the Holy Spirit's impulse.

From this dangerous position we will not receive the life-giving touch of the Holy Spirit, but will receive only "imaginations." We will imagine that God is speaking to us and we are receiving direction from heaven. Our mind is very capable of deceiving us. Many people are deceived, thinking God is speaking to them. The one who doesn't have daily communion with the heart of the Father will be a victim of imaginations and false visions. This is the reason why so many people run to crusades, concerts, services, or conferences; they're searching for God's direction through men and women who hear the voice of God.

PRAY AS JESUS PRAYED

JESUS' PRAYER SHOULD be our prayer also. John 17 presents seven requests of Jesus on our behalf:

1. That the Father be glorified in the glorification of His Son, Jesus (v. 1).

My prayer: Father, glorify Jesus our Savior in my family; save my loved ones. Glorify Yourself by glorifying Jesus the Physician, Provider, Liberator, and the Anointed One. Father, I will wait until Jesus is glorified.

2. For the restoration of the eternal glory of the Son (v. 5).

My prayer: Lord Jesus, nothing on this earth can compare to Your glory. My eyes are fixed on the glory You will possess one day. Satan, his angels, and all the kingdoms of this earth have only a temporary glory. Father, even though my needs are real, my heart waits for the day when Jesus will reign over all in glory and power. Jesus, You are Lord!

*3. For the protection of the believers in the world
from the evil one (vv. 11, 15).*

My prayer: Lord, in this very moment You are praying for
my protection and my security. I'm not afraid because whatever You ask of the Father is granted.

*4. For the sanctification of the believers
by the Word and truth (v. 17).*

My prayer: Lord, we are not to search the Scriptures by
obligation. Today I read and study Your Word because it is
truth, and that truth sanctifies me. Father, revive Your Word
in my heart and highlight some biblical principle that I have
studied, heard, or read. Father, in this prayer I seek the
truth, Your truth.

5. For the spiritual unity of the believers (v. 21).

My prayer: Lord, make us one. Just as You and the Father
are one, make me one with my brothers and sisters, even if
they are from another race or nationality. Father, tear out
my selfish thoughts. Father, heal us!

6. For the world to believe in Jesus (v. 21).

My prayer: Lord, I don't pray for the growth of the
church. I pray that everybody will believe in You. You are
the Savior of the world. Father, glorify Jesus in the nations!
Use me to bring glory to the Son.

*7. For the believers to be able to be with Christ
and to see His glory (v. 24).*

My prayer: Lord, come soon. I am waiting for You. Nothing
in this earth matters to me anymore. Thank You for preparing
a place for me. Thank You for creating a paradise for me.

Nine

PRAISE THAT PREVAILS

W HEN A PERSON turns his or her heart to God without making a pact with the natural mind, he or she will experience resistance. The natural, the human, and the carnal will always oppose the work of the Holy Spirit. The Bible warns us about this. (See Romans 8:7, KJV.)

True worshipers make other people uncomfortable. They are too transparent, too direct, and not diplomatic enough. Their only commitment is to the heart of God. Not everyone who worships has this same commitment. A great number of Christians don't know the heart of God. They are easily led by what the majority says, by tradition, and by what seems convenient. When a true worshiper starts to talk, many Christians don't understand him and thus resist his words. This has always happened and will continue to happen, although it may look different every time.

From the very first day of my personal renewal, God started to renew the radio station's employees also. The programs changed. The music changed. The way of ministering changed. And God didn't stop there—the listeners began to experience the same thing. Many times as I sat alone in the studio, worshiping the Lord on a live broadcast, the Holy Spirit would talk to me, touch me, point things out to me, and comfort me. At the same time that the Holy Spirit was ministering to me, miraculously He was also touching thousands of people who were listening to our broadcast.

Many leaders, lay leaders, friends, and coworkers didn't understand. Because many people who testified on the air and in their churches included my name in their testimonies, my name started to resound. Some people accused me of wanting to raise myself up as a prophet over the city, projecting my own ministry and searching for fame and renown. Others accused me of having a financial interest in the promotion of the worship music we used on the air.

Other unfounded accusations started to appear. I was accused of not teaching the people how to purify themselves externally, speaking only of inner purity. Others accused me of being "worldly" and "liberal."

We began holding praise and worship services. Our meetings are probably different than other meetings. Everything we do is directed to Jesus. We do not promote on the radio the people who participate in the services. We simply prepare an organized program and submit it to the Holy Spirit's will.

Following the pattern of Psalm 100:4, we start every celebration with joyful music, coming before Him with thanksgiving. These are joyful, elated moments. We have every reason to be happy. Our God is a living God, and He is our Father. Our Father delights in us. He has provided a Savior, and His name is *Jesus.* Our Father has sent us a Comforter, the Holy Spirit, who doesn't dwell in buildings, but in us. We are accepted in the Beloved, Christ Jesus. Although we know that on this earth we will go through afflictions, we also know God has given us many beautiful promises in which we can completely trust.

During worship, the Holy Spirit makes His presence known to us. He manifests Himself in every life that glorifies and exalts the Son of God, Jesus Christ. As the presence of the Holy Spirit becomes tangible, the Spirit begins to speak, to reason, and to comfort. This is the time to worship, repent, and surrender. The music changes. The atmosphere changes. We enter into worship when we surrender our hearts to God for Him to do with as He pleases. After we preach the Word, we end by going back to worship.

These final moments are crucial. People have been confronted with the Word of God, and it is now time to make a decision. We have discovered that if we challenge people right after the message, many only respond emotionally. But if we give people a few minutes to meditate, they make wise, heartfelt decisions. After a time of worship, people surrender themselves at the feet of Christ and receive an immediate deliverance.

In the first praise and worship service, more than two thousand people attended; hundreds were unable to get into the meeting hall. That was amazing, since we didn't have a special guest. The people came to be in the manifest presence of God. Since then we have been leading praise and worship services to our Lord in the biggest auditoriums of the metropolitan area of New York, and we have been leading crusades in various Latin American countries several times a year. Thousands have given their lives to our Lord Jesus, and many others have experienced renewal in their spiritual lives. In addition, the Holy Spirit has performed amazing miracles in the lives of many of the people.

In September 1996, after a week of prayer and fasting, we felt compelled to begin planning for a ten-day prayer and fasting retreat with the entire radio station staff. In October of that same year, the entire staff, close to forty people, met each day at 11 A.M. in the conference room to pray and seek the manifest presence of God. From the very first day, the Holy Spirit came over us with deep repentance. We spent hours crying and groaning, asking forgiveness from God and from our coworkers. The next day, during a live radio program, the Holy Spirit's conviction hit us; we started to repent publicly for all the mistakes we had made and the worldly techniques we had used to raise funds during the radio marathons. The radio audience realized that something different was happening in the radio station, and hundreds of people came down to the station to spend the day praying with us.

When we left the studio, there were hundreds of people in the corridors, the lobby, and all over the building. We decided to lead a worship service. We continued for ten consecutive days. The Lord manifested His presence in awesome ways. One afternoon, a busload of fifty men from a local church came to the service at the station. As they walked into the building, the Holy Spirit fell on them, and they all started to cry in a loud voice. When I heard the cries, I went to investigate; I saw half of the group flattened against one wall and the other half stuck against the opposite wall as if they were being held against those walls. There they remained for more than an hour and a half. Whoever passed down the hall between them or even looked at them received the same spirit of brokenness.

In those ten days, God came. Souls who came into our building uninvited were converted. Christians who came to receive from God left renewed. Through our live broadcast, local and international radio listeners were receiving the same impartation. Many lives were transformed. At the end of those ten days, the crowd could not fit into our building.

On the last day I told everybody that we would continue meeting in a church building. We immediately received a phone call from the president of the radio station's Board of Directors, telling me to stop those prayer services. Denominational leaders were afraid this would become a movement, a church, and people would start following me as their leader, abandoning their congregations. With deep sorrow, we had to announce that we couldn't continue the meetings. God had come, and we had received Him for only a little while.

I was never able to understand the criticism. Unbelievers were saved. People who had gone astray came back to the church. The sick were healed. Believers experienced a spiritual revival. The oppressed were delivered. *Why so much criticism? Why so much distrust?* I wanted to understand my critics, but God wanted to show me the purpose of it all.

God answered my questions clearly: I needed to learn to praise God!

I couldn't understand this. I come from a Pentecostal background. If there's a church that knows how to praise, it's a Pentecostal church. I thought I knew how to praise God. But when I had to face opposition, then I understood what real praise is all about.

Praise has been a very important part of Christian church liturgy. Evangelicals have understood praise as an activity that brings joy and happiness to our congregations. In thousands of churches around the world and in hundreds of Christian activities, the congregation is exhorted to praise God. Words such as "lift your hands," "declare the greatness and wonders of God," "sing aloud," "shout," "jump," and "smile" are used to lead the congregation in physical and verbal actions called "praise." The more shouting, the more singing, and the less silence there is, the more intense the praise is believed to be.

But, what happens to praise when problems and false accusations hit? What happens when a loved one is lost or when we experience disappointments? What happens when we shout, sing, and dance in "praise," but the burden doesn't go?

This is what was happening to me. In the most glorious moment of my life, I was facing an opposition that was taking my joy away. And so I wondered: *If I am doing God's will, if I am growing spiritually, if my heart is, for the very first time, turned to God with all my strength, why such opposition?*

During those days of uncertainty, I felt a strong urge to begin a verse-by-verse Bible study of Hebrews in the Sunday school class I lead at the church I attend. While studying the circumstances of this particular Christian community to whom the letter was addressed, I found the following:

- These Hebrews were a community of Jews who had accepted Jesus as Savior and Messiah.

- As Christians, they didn't offer animal sacrifices at the temple in Jerusalem, which was still standing.

- The religious orthodox Jews had organized a campaign of violent persecution against these believers. Many Christians had been put in jail, and others were going through very difficult trials.

- Due to the persecution, some of the Christian Jews were thinking about the possibility of returning to the Jewish temple to offer sacrifices according to their traditions.

- The writer of Hebrews sent this epistle to encourage the believers to continue to "fix [their] eyes on Jesus, the author and perfecter of [their] faith" (12:2).

What a difficult situation! However, in the midst of this painful persecution, the writer says:

> Keep on loving each other as brothers. Do not forget to entertain strangers, for by so doing some people have entertained angels without knowing it. Remember those in prison as if you were their fellow prisoners, and those who are mistreated as if you yourselves were suffering.... Keep your lives free from the love of money and be content with what you have, because God has said, "Never will I leave you; never will I forsake you." So we say with confidence, "The Lord is my helper; I will not be afraid. What can man do to me?"...Jesus Christ is the same yesterday and today and forever.
>
> —HEBREWS 13:1–3, 5–6, 8

The writer goes on to explain:

We have an altar. . . . Let us, then, go to him outside the camp, bearing the disgrace he bore. . . . Through Jesus, therefore, let us continually offer to God a sacrifice of praise—the fruit of lips that confess his name. And do not forget to do good and to share with others, for with such sacrifices God is pleased.

—HEBREWS 13:10, 13, 15–16

The Hebrew Christians were losing their jobs, their social standing, and their material goods. Yet the writer exhorts them to love one another with brotherly love and to take care of each other's needs. He tells them not to be greedy, to be free from the love of money. The will of God was that they would not be in the habit of loving material goods. They were to be "content" with what they had, a very commendable attitude, but an impossible one unless they considered the full context of his words.

"I AM WITH YOU"

IN THIS SAME chapter of Hebrews, the writer quotes the promise God made to Jacob as he was running away from his brother Esau, and to Joshua before entering into the Promised Land, and to Solomon as he sat on the throne of his father David (Heb. 13:5–6.).

God promised Jacob that the presence of God would go with him wherever he went (Gen. 28:13–15). In Hebrew, the word *presence* also means "face" or "countenance." The implication was that God would walk in front of Jacob, not looking ahead but looking toward Jacob who needed His protection. God walks ahead of us, with His face always turned toward us, His children. God's countenance isn't directed toward the blessing, toward the solution to our problems. The face of God is turned toward us. God is more interested in us than in the solution to our earthly problems: "The LORD . . . observes the sons of men; his eyes examine them. The LORD examines the righteous" (Ps. 11:4–5).

The righteous and just will contemplate the face of God, because God always examines the righteous and just man.

"NEVER WILL I LEAVE YOU"

A LITERAL TRANSLATION of this text would be: "No, never, certainly not, there's no way I would ever let go of your hand. I would never let you sink; I would never stop supporting you." The verb expresses that there isn't the faintest possibility He would ever leave us.

"NEVER WILL I FORSAKE YOU"

HERE GOD USES a negative again. A literal translation could be: "No, no, certainly not, there's no way I would abandon you, leave you in a difficult situation without help, or leave you when you were dying." There is no possibility of God's ever forsaking us.

This is a promise we can proclaim with confidence and encouragement: God is our helper. The original text implies "he who runs to help, to succor the needy." If God runs when we need help, let us not be afraid of what man can do to us. This promise was given for those Christian Hebrews who were under the threat of religious men who had the ability to destroy their lives and their families. They wanted to force the Christians to go back to the tradition at the altar of sacrifices at the temple. They were threatening them even with death. This is the same spirit that had already manifested in the persecutions in Jerusalem after Stephen's martyrdom. Paul and the missionary apostles were continually suffering at the hands of religious militants.

The writer of the Book of Hebrews tells them not to be afraid because there was another altar—the altar on which Jesus had been sacrificed. That altar was not in the temple, because it was Jesus Himself, our helper, the One who is the same yesterday, today, and forever. When we come to the altar, we can't come with empty hands. The purpose of going to the altar is to present a sacrifice, to offer something of value, to give away something that is precious to us. On the altar, we present an offering. On the altar that is Jesus Christ Himself, we need to offer a sacrifice.

How do we go to that altar? Bearing the "disgrace" of Jesus, the defamation and the shame that Christ endured during His passion and His death on the cross. Jesus Christ didn't try to run away from suffering. He didn't experience joy when He had to carry the cross, suffer the beatings, and go through the death on the cross. He was presenting a sacrifice, and at the same time He contemplated the joy set before Him—the Resurrection and the glory of the throne at the right hand of God the Father.

According to Hebrews 13:15, the sacrifice that must be offered is no longer an animal, human efforts, or ceremonies. It is a sacrifice of praise, the fruit of lips that confess the name of Jesus the Messiah, He who never changes, our helper, He who will never leave us nor forsake us. In Him is our faith.

The process is as follows:

- I consider my miserable situation, my "disgrace."
- I am content with what I presently have because my heart is thankful to Christ for my salvation and the promise of eternal life.
- I offer the fruit of my lips, a sacrifice of praise to Jesus, who is unchangeable.

One doesn't praise in order to feel joy. *Praise is a sacrifice.* When we praise simply to experience joy, to feel better, or so everyone can say we had a wonderful experience, we are not presenting a sacrifice. Praise is a sacrifice to Jesus, our Savior and King. It has nothing to do with what we feel; it has to do with the greatness and the faithfulness of God.

Praise is one of the most powerful weapons available to the Christian. In a war, a soldier doesn't stop to ask himself if he feels like fighting. When the enemy is advancing, the soldier resists and fights. When we are in the midst of a conflict, we are not very joyful. It is, however, the moment to praise, or to fight.

In the Book of Judges, we are told about the conquest of the Promised Land. After the death of the great leader Joshua, there was still much territory to conquer. The land of Canaan was occupied by the Canaanites. God had removed His people from Egypt, had protected them in the desert, and had taken them to the Promised Land. The promise was clear. The land belonged to them. Now they had to take possession of it.

The Book of Judges tells us that "after the death of Joshua, the Israelites asked the LORD, 'Who will be the first to go up and fight for us against the Canaanites?' The LORD answered, 'Judah is to go; I have given the land into their hands'" (Judg. 1:1–2).

God ordered Judah to fight. *Judah* means "praise." Judah was Jacob's fourth son. Before he died, Jacob blessed *Judah* (that is, *Praise*) with these words:

> Judah, your brothers will praise you;
>> your hand will be on the neck of your enemies;
>> your father's sons will bow down to you.
> You are a lion's cub, O Judah;
>> you return from the prey, my son.
> Like a lion he crouches and lies down,
>> like a lioness—who dares to rouse him?
> The scepter will not depart from Judah,
>> nor the ruler's staff from between his feet,
> until he comes to whom it belongs
>> and the obedience of the nations is his.
>> —GENESIS 49:8–10

The blessing of Jacob is aggressive, militant, and victorious. David declared: "Yet, the LORD, the God of Israel, chose me from my whole family to be king over Israel forever. He chose Judah [Praise] as leader" (1 Chron. 28:4).

When the people of Israel marched through the desert, Judah (Praise) was in the front, leading. Judah was marching with his face toward the Promised Land, and God was guiding Israel with His presence.

Judah's banner was the figure of a lion's cub. In his blessing to his son, Jacob had told him that he, Judah (Praise), was like a lion—when he crouched and lay down, no one dared to rouse him. The scepter of authority was in the hands of Judah, in the hands of Praise. When the Israelites reached the border of Canaan, they sent spies into the land. Caleb went as a representative of Praise. When they had to fight, God always sent Praise before them.

> In Judah God is known;
>> his name is great in Israel.
> His tent is in Salem,
>> his dwelling place in Zion.
> There he broke the flashing arrows,
>> the shields and the swords, the weapons of war.
>> —PSALM 76:1–3

God is known in Judah (Praise): God manifests Himself in the praise. There, God breaks the arrows, the shields, the swords, and all the weapons of the enemy.

Psalm 149 explains that praise is not a battle in which one tries to defeat the enemy. Rather, praise imposes obedience on enemies that are defeated already.

> Sing to the LORD a new song [fresh, just reaped],
>> his praise [song, melody] in the assembly of the saints.

> Let Israel rejoice [gleam, shine] in their Maker [Creator and constant sustainer];
>> let the people of Zion be glad [spin around] in their King.

143

Let them praise [with boasting, ostentation, and brag-
ging] his name [honor, authority, character, and
position] with dancing
and make music [sing with instrumental accompani-
ment] to him with tambourine and harp.
For the LORD takes delight [pleasure, satisfaction] in his
people;
he crowns [ornates, decorates] the humble [crushed]
with salvation [*Yeshua:* liberation, help, victory,
prosperity].
Let the saints rejoice [jump, leap] in this honor
and sing [shout aloud] for joy on their beds [place of
rest].

May the praise [exaltation, elevation, raised up high] of
God be in their mouths
and a double-edged sword in their hands...
—PSALM 149:1–6

The psalmist definitely is telling us to praise. Therefore
we are to:

- Sing a new song.
- Praise with melodies.
- Rejoice.
- Boast about His name.
- Sing accompanied by musical instruments.
- Leap with joy.
- Sing, shout aloud, and scream.

These are the external manifestations of praise. In verse
6, we see that praise exalts God by declaring that He is
higher and loftier than any circumstance. God is higher than
death, than the tomb, than any pain or disappointment.
God is above any governor on this earth, any expert, any
organization, any threat from men. God is higher, loftier,
and more elevated than Satan, than his whole hellish army,

than any religion, pact, or agreement.

How do we exalt God? With our mouths. Whom do we exalt? Only Him. Many people use their mouths to exalt their own problems. Others exalt Satan. The man who praises exalts and lifts up God with his mouth.

Some say it isn't necessary to praise the Lord so much. Others say they praise God in private, in their minds, and in their hearts. Praise cannot be confined to our minds: We have to express it with our mouth. Why? Because our enemy is not all-knowing, and he needs to be reminded that in this battle, the children of God are victorious in Christ. In this battle, God's children don't make use of mental, psychological, or religious weapons. Our weapon, as children of God, is to praise at the top of our voices.

Hebrews 4:12 declares that the Word of God is sharper than a double-edged sword. Notice carefully where this powerful, sharp, and devastating Word of God is found. It is in our hands. It is not in our mouth; there we find only praises exalting God. The hands represent what we do, our behavior, what we produce in our lives, and our testimony. The Word of God has to be present in our testimony. What good is it to declare the Word of God if we are not applying it to our daily lives? When we combine the Word of God with His commandments and the praise that flows from our mouth, we are fighting a victorious spiritual battle.

Ephesians 6:17 says, "Take...the sword of the Spirit, which is the word of God."

When praise is in our mouths, the Holy Spirit takes it and fights for us. Notice that the Word of God is not *our* sword. The Word of God is the sword *of the Spirit*. He is the only one who knows how to use it. Consequently, we should not arm ourselves for battle; we should depend totally on the Holy Spirit to do it for us. In other words, we should allow Him to select the Scriptures with which we are to fight. If we, with the arm or the mind of flesh, begin indiscriminately wielding Bible verses, we will injure people. The battle is the Lord's.

In the church, the Bible has been used as a sword to needlessly inflict hurt. The sad result is that hundreds of denominations, theological groups, and traditions believe their individual group has the only true biblical doctrine. The Bible has been used to divide, isolate, offend, and wound. People have taken a sword that they don't know how to handle and have done much harm.

There is good news! The Holy Spirit is restoring praise in the mouth of the church and is healing the wounds of those mouths that are empty of praise and full of pride.

The enemy is behind every conflict in our lives. We are at war when we face difficulties in the world, at home, in the church, or within our circle of friends. All these struggles need to be confronted with spiritual weapons.

The first reaction when facing any type of attack has to be praise. With praise on our lips and the Word of God in our way of living, we will defeat His enemies and any sin that could manifest in His family, the church. When we exalt God, we don't have time to speak against our enemies. We don't criticize or analyze the reasons, the strategies, or the motivations of those who are opposing us. We are too busy exalting God.

Our testimony has to be an attack weapon. We have to be careful not to leave any places uncovered where the enemy can accuse us and establish a stronghold. Our testimony has to be solid, without any breaches. If there are breaches in your testimony, if there are offenses and wounds, confess them to God and to those you have offended; close that gap.

When we obey the Word of God in our daily walk, no one should accuse us:

> The spiritual man makes judgments about all things,
> but he himself is not subject to any man's judgment:
> "For who has known the mind of the Lord that he may
> instruct him?" But we have the mind of Christ.
> —1 CORINTHIANS 2:15–16

Nobody can launch a successful judgment verdict against a spiritual man who constantly exalts God with the Word in his hands and daily life. Do you know what happens when someone tries? The attacker gets confused and tired and eventually leaves. He can't find a target for which to aim. The more criticism the attacker levels, the more praise comes forth. Rather than ignoring the enemy, the spiritual man confronts him with weapons he cannot resist.

> ...to bind [put a yoke on, tighten the reins] their kings [seated on a throne] with fetters [ties], their nobles [honored] with shackles of iron.
>
> —PSALM 149:8

This response is the result of praise. The enthroned enemies are bound, and their henchmen are controlled with shackles of iron. Our battle is not against individuals, but against spiritual forces, against kings or rulers, against nobles or powers in the heavenly realms.

> ...to carry out the sentence [verdict decreed by the Judge] written [recorded and filed] against them.
>
> —PSALM 149:9

Praise brings the verdict of the Judge into effect. What is the verdict over these kings? What verdict has God put into the hands of those who praise Him? Judah was a lion's cub, but two thousand years ago the Lion of the tribe of Judah came, and the cross of Calvary conquered powers and authorities, as announced by Paul in his letter to the Colossians:

> When you were dead in your sins and in the uncircumcision of your sinful nature, God made you alive with Christ. He forgave us all our sins, having canceled the written code, with its regulations, that was against us and that stood opposed to us; he took it away, nailing

it to the cross. And having disarmed the powers and authorities, he made a public spectacle of them, triumphing over them by the cross.

—COLOSSIANS 2:13–15

In Paul's words, the imposition of this verdict is:

Therefore do not let anyone judge you by what you eat or drink, or with regard to a religious festival, a New Moon celebration or a Sabbath day. These are a shadow of the things that were to come; the reality, however, is found in Christ. Do not let anyone who delights in false humility and the worship of angels disqualify you for the prize. Such a person goes into great detail about what he has seen, and his unspiritual mind puffs him up with idle notions. He has lost connection with the Head....

Since you died with Christ to the basic principles of this world, why, as though you still belonged to it, do you submit to its rules: "Do not handle! Do not taste! Do not touch!"...Such regulations indeed have an appearance of wisdom, with their self-imposed worship, their false humility and their harsh treatment of the body, but they lack any value in restraining sensual indulgence.

—COLOSSIANS 2:16–23

What is God's verdict in our hands?

- We have the life of Christ.
- All our sins have been forgiven.
- There is no written code against the believer.
- There is no condemnation for those who are in Christ Jesus.
- The principalities and powers have been "disarmed."
- The principalities and powers have been publicly shamed.

Jesus Christ triumphed over them by the cross. From that day on they have been defeated.

Therefore, our prize, our recompense, is secure in Christ. We don't have to win it through our own "religious" efforts, as the Pharisees used to claim. They couldn't come close to a Gentile, touch objects previously handled by Gentiles, or eat what Gentiles ate. How sad it is that these things are still being taught in certain Christian circles! There are still thousands of believers who are trying fervently to gain the recompense that Christ has reserved in heaven for those who simply accept Him by faith.

Has the enemy tried to present to you an accusation that makes you doubt God's verdict in your life? Has the enemy tried to accuse you of sin, of violating God's law? Has the enemy "preached" to you, telling you that you are not doing enough to please God? Has the enemy condemned you, telling you that you are not sufficiently holy? Have you been left depressed? Has the enemy introduced himself as an invincible and boastful being, threatening that you will end up defeated? Let me tell you that those who worship God enforce the verdict Christ consummated at the cross of Calvary.

During wartime, the troops who launch the first assault against the enemy's positions are trained to attack, destroy, and defeat the enemy. After the victory is achieved, the assault troops retreat, and the occupation forces arrive. The army in charge of the occupation doesn't have to fight because the enemy has been already defeated. The occupation army's responsibility is to keep the territory that has been captured.

Christ assaulted the gates of hell and death. He obtained the victory when He was resurrected and ascended to heaven to sit at the right hand of the Father. In the process, He shamed and disarmed the principalities, which together with the powers of the enemy tried to prevent the work of Christ. However, Christ won, went through the heavens, and humiliated them publicly. We don't have to fight any longer. We just have to take possession of the promises that belong to us. How? By exalting Christ with our mouths and putting into practice the Word of God.

In 2 Chronicles 20, we are told about the events concerning the people of Judah, the people of Praise, as they were surrounded by a vast army of men from Moab, Ammon, and Mount Seir. Notice some of the enemies' characteristics.

- *Moab and Ammon were descendants of Lot, Abraham's nephew.* Moab was the fruit of the incestuous relationship between Lot and his eldest daughter. The Moabites and Ammonites were children of sin and rebellion. (Don't be surprised when friends, relatives, or coworkers attack you.)

- *The people of Mount Seir were the Edomites, descendants of Esau, Jacob's brother.* Esau rejected the blessing. Esau was a man interested in earthly things. (Don't be surprised when you are tempted to compromise your principles.)

- *The Moabites and the Ammonites worshiped the god Moloch and offered human sacrifices to him, especially children.* (Don't be surprised when the enemy tries to steal your family from you.)

- *The territory of Moab was just on the other side of the Promised Land's border.* They weren't distant enemies. They were quite close. (Don't expect an attack from strangers; the enemy can attack through your family, friends, or people in your church.)

- *On their way to Canaan, the Moabites and Ammonites hired the services of a prophet named Balaam so he would curse Israel.* (Don't be surprised when some "prophets" prophesy disasters or curse what God has declared blessed.)

- *On their way to Canaan, the people of Edom didn't give Israel permission to march through their territory, making their journey much harder.* (Don't be surprised when difficulties arise, hindering God's vision from being accomplished in your life.)

- *These three nations were a constant irritation to God's people.* They were defeated by the judges, by Saul, by David, and by Jehoshaphat; but they always seemed to reappear after some time. (Don't be surprised if, after a while, the same problems show up again.)

- *These three enemies marched against King Jehoshaphat and the people of Judah (Praise).* Jehoshaphat summoned the people to a big prayer service, and standing before all the people of Judah (Praise), he called out to God saying:

  See how they are repaying us by coming to drive us out of the possession you gave us as an inheritance.
  —2 Chronicles 20:11

The enemy will always try to steal from us that which God has already given us. (Take careful notice of what he is saying: Satan wants to take something from you that God has already given to you—your inheritance.) Jehoshaphat added:

  O our God, will you not judge them? For we have no power to face this vast army that is attacking us. We do not know what to do, but our eyes are upon you.
  —2 Chronicles 20:12

Jehoshaphat recalled the original covenant between God and Abraham and his descendants. He didn't cry or ask in desperation. God had already promised the land to Israel as an inheritance, and no thief could claim it.

All Judah was standing before the Lord, listening to King Jehoshaphat's prayer. Suddenly, as they were praising and worshiping God, the Holy Spirit fell on the Levites. The Holy Spirit, the Comforter, manifests His presence and His comforting direction whenever there is a group of worshipers who have taken their eyes away from the disaster that surrounds them and turned them to God. The Holy Spirit always provides direction and peace when a worshiper confesses that although he doesn't know what to do, his trust is in the Lord.

The Holy Spirit said:

> Listen, King Jehoshaphat and all who live in Judah and Jerusalem! This is what the LORD says to you: "Do not be afraid or discouraged because of this vast army. For the battle is not yours, but God's."
>
> —2 CHRONICLES 20:15

The Holy Spirit then instructed the people of Judah how to prepare themselves for the great victory. He revealed the secret plans of the enemy—where they would be climbing up and where they would be staying. He declared that Judah would not have to fight; they just had to take up their positions, stand firm, and see the deliverance of God. When the people heard such clear instructions, Jehoshaphat and all the people of Judah (people of Praise) fell down in worship before the Lord and praised the Lord, the God of Israel, with a "very loud voice" (2 Chron. 20:18–19). Then the people of Judah went to sleep. The solution was not in their hands—the battle was the Lord's.

The story continues:

> Early in the morning they left for the Desert of Tekoa. As they set out, Jehoshaphat stood and said, "Listen to me, Judah and people of Jerusalem! Have faith in the LORD your God and you will be upheld; have faith in his prophets and you will be successful." After con-

sulting the people, Jehoshaphat appointed men to sing to the Lord and to praise him for the splendor of his holiness as they went out at the head of the army, saying: "Give thanks to the Lord, for his love endures forever."

—2 Chronicles 20:20–21

What were the worshipers doing? They were exalting and glorifying God. They were declaring that God was loftier, more extolled than His enemies. God was going to glorify His name, not because Judah deserved it, but because of His goodness and mercy. There was worship on their lips, and they believed the Holy Spirit's instructions received through the prophets. They believed God's Word, and now they were going into action.

As they began to sing and praise, the Lord set ambushes against the men of Ammon and Moab and Mount Seir who were invading Judah, and they were defeated.

—2 Chronicles 20:22

The ambushes that were meant to destroy the people of Judah became their enemies' tomb! God fought for Judah. God gave the people of Praise the victory over their enemies.

But this is not the end of it. God ordered the Israelites to prepare to encounter the enemy—not to fight, but to plunder them.

So Jehoshaphat and his men went to carry off their plunder, and they found among them a great amount of equipment and clothing and also articles of value— more than they could take away.

—2 Chronicles 20:25

What is the purpose of our battle against the devil, the world, and our flesh? To plunder the enemy, to take the

153

lives he holds in prison away from him.

Thousands of Christians suffer the pain of being the only ones saved in their families. Maybe you are one of them, and you feel like Jehoshaphat, without any strength and without knowing what to do. Praise God! Exalt Him! He is more powerful than the forces that hold your family in bondage. Live a life according to God's Word in their presence. God will give you the victory to come in and plunder the enemy. In that ruined life, you will find booty of precious gems for the glory of God.

Many Christians will have to practice this in their jobs, neighborhoods, and schools. God is calling His church to be like Judah (Praise). We have the scepter of authority; let's march in the name of Jesus, the victorious one. Never exalt a problem. Never exalt the work of the enemy. Your enemy has been shamed.

Is there any joy in the praise? Of course!

> Then, led by Jehoshaphat, all the men of Judah and Jerusalem returned joyfully to Jerusalem, for the LORD had given them cause to rejoice over their enemies. They entered Jerusalem and went to the temple of the LORD with harps and lutes and trumpets. The fear of God came upon all the kingdoms of the countries when they heard how the LORD had fought against the enemies of Israel.
>
> —2 CHRONICLES 20:27–29

Joy comes when God gives it to us; it is a fruit of the Spirit—not a product of our emotions, the music, or our enthusiasm. Joy comes when God acts, when we obey His Word, when we exalt Him, and when we plunder the enemy.

This was an episode in the life of the people of Judah, the people of Praise. This is how God deals with those who worship Him. God did this with me, and He continues to do it with others. We don't have time to analyze what the enemy is scheming, but the Holy Spirit knows all his tricks. In His time, He will warn, counsel, and guide us. Turn your eyes to the Lord and exalt Him before His altar of the sacrifice of praise. Your enemy is powerful, and he is rich. However, don't worry; the richer he gets, the bigger the plunder will be.

As a minister who is constantly preaching in Latin America, I used to compare what God was doing there with what He was doing in the church in North America and other English-speaking countries. If we compare, the conclusions are depressing. But in these last months, the Holy Spirit has been revealing His heart through music and messages. Most of the worship music I hear celebrates the great manifestation of divine glory over the church in North America, Great Britain, and Oceania. The anointed messages of prophets, teachers, and pastors speak of an imminent revival of which we already perceive the first signs. I don't compare anymore. Now I worship God for what will be manifesting over the nations. Yes, it is true that sin abounds. However, the last harvest is coming, not only for Third World countries, but also for the whole world. Praise the Lord! The more sin and evil, the greater the manifestation of power and glory will be and the greater the harvest.

Ten

THE POWER OF REVELATION

ONE AFTERNOON AFTER a pastor's conference, I met a young man who had hopes of entering the ministry. I was holding in my hands a devotional book somebody had just given me. As we were talking, I felt the young man was extremely confused about his calling. He told me about his plans and his ambitions. He also told me about the problems in his church. He seemed to have an answer for everything.

I wanted to give him the devotional book I had in my hands. I offered it to him, but he refused. He told me he preferred to read technical books (theology and biblical commentaries) that would give him a better knowledge of God's Word. He reminded me of the way I used to be. I didn't like devotional books. I'd rather read and study biblical commentaries and analyses of biblical texts in their original languages. For me, devotional books were too mystical and subjective. They were descriptions of personal experiences of holy men and women who had been called to a life of *holiness*. I wanted to be an intellectual. I wanted *knowledge*.

INTELLECTUAL KNOWLEDGE ALONE

MANY HAVE TAUGHT on the importance of biblical knowledge, including myself. Many exhort people to memorize Bible passages. Although study and memorization are vital in the life of a Christian, they will never produce change. The Holy Spirit produces change.

I used to read the Bible because it was my work manual. For me, the Bible was a source of study, knowledge, information, and truth. Biblical knowledge gave me credibility and authority. There are many who are impressed by people with knowledge, titles, and education. Therefore, I was determined to study, to know the Bible and any biblical material that would help me to become a knowledgeable man. I wanted to be a man with a deep knowledge of the Bible like my professors in the Christian university and seminary.

But all my knowledge was purely intellectual. What was my problem? I didn't have an intimate relationship with either my Father or the Holy Spirit. It is very difficult to learn in depth about someone we don't know intimately.

We can find an example of the desire for intellectual knowledge in the first temptation of man. The temptation was directed to the human desire to obtain and possess. Satan appealed to the desire to obtain knowledge. I'm not saying this is wrong. To obtain an education and knowledge is a good thing. However, Adam wanted to obtain it without submitting to God or depending upon Him who is the only source of all wisdom. Satan presented knowledge as something good. But behind the desire for knowledge existed the motivation to obtain knowledge in order to dominate and subdue. We must all examine our motives for knowing more about God. Are you studying the Word because you want to teach others—or because you want to make a name for yourself? If you are still struggling with your motivations, with your desire to obtain a position through knowledge, remember this: Satan hasn't changed his strategy—and the human heart hasn't changed either.

RENEW ME

God Wants to Renew Us

I HAD FALLEN into the trap of seeking to obtain intellectual knowledge for personal gain. A theological education appeared as something good, but behind that good intention was a demonic temptation. This is the reason why so many who know so much about God show no evidence of it in their personal relationships with their families, churches, and communities. Only an intimate relationship *with* God—not knowledge *about* God—will change the world.

God had to change me as He changed Abraham.

Abraham asked God for something: Wholeheartedly, he wanted to have a son. That son would give him notoriety (Gen. 15:2). But after Abraham had an encounter with the Lord, he only asked God for His presence (Gen. 18:3). He didn't *want something from Him;* he only *wanted God.*

I had a personal encounter with the Holy Spirit. After God renewed my life of worship, then He renewed my study and knowledge of His Word. A hunger for God awakened in me; since then I'm continually being renewed from glory to glory. In the days following that initial experience, the Holy Spirit brought me into a deeper knowledge of Jesus Christ, my Lord and my King. Through worship, the presence of Jesus Christ became very real and palpable to me.

I remember one morning during the radio worship program I started to talk about the invitation made by Jesus during the Feast of Tabernacles. He said, "If anyone is thirsty, let him come to me and drink. Whoever believes in me, as the Scripture has said, streams of living water will flow from within him" (John 7:37–38).

As I concluded this simple teaching, I sensed the Holy Spirit wanted to manifest His glorious presence in our midst. As we continued to worship, the Holy Spirit's glorious presence was manifested in people who were listening to us, not only in our studios, but also in homes, offices, and cars. I didn't want to leave the studio.

I've had many experiences like this. The glory of God is so real! Even though He is omnipresent, His glory doesn't manifest just anywhere, but only in places separated and prepared for Him to dwell: places of praise and worship. The holy God abides, is enthroned, and reigns in the praises of His people.

For those who tell me that they don't need experiences, that the Word of God is all they need—you are right! This is correct. But allow me to share my heart with you. After my initial renewal experience, the Word of God prompted me to seek God even more. Through the experiences of biblical men and women who were transformed by their encounters with God, the Holy Spirit challenged me to desire the same thing for my life.

Why do you think the experience Isaiah described in the sixth chapter of the Book of Isaiah is in the Bible? Why do you think the experiences of Moses, Abraham, David, Jesus, and the apostles are recorded in the Bible? Just for our knowledge? I don't think so. They are there as our example, so that we can imitate them. Yes, it is true we won't receive any further revelation than what God has already given through the Bible, but *we* can expect to receive the same revelations as were given to the men and women of the Bible.

> Yet you are enthroned as the Holy One; you are the praise of Israel.
>
> —PSALM 22:3

> I have seen you in the sanctuary and beheld your power and your glory.
>
> —PSALM 63:2

THE GLORY OF GOD IN JARS OF CLAY

THE HOLY GOD dwells and is contemplated in the sanctuary.

The *sanctuary* is a place that has been set apart, properly purified, and consecrated so that God's presence may be manifested in it. The glory of God was in the holy of holies, in Moses' tabernacle, and in Jerusalem's temple. Since Christ's ascension to the heavens and the coming of the Holy Spirit in Pentecost, the glory of God does not abide in buildings, tents, or any ceremonial utensils any longer. The glory of God now abides in jars of clay—our lives and our bodies.

When the glory of God started to manifest every time I worshiped and prayed, a deep hunger for searching God's Word arose within me. I wasn't interested in technical knowledge or biblical interpretation any longer—I was interested in knowing God. I was interested in knowing His ways. The Holy Spirit was placing in me a care and a sensibility toward what pleases and displeases God. I had always known that worship, praise, prayer, reading His Word, and serving others are things that are pleasing to Him. But now it was different. In the intimacy of worship and prayer, I sensed I had to worship in a manner acceptable to Him, according to His ways and designs.

That desire was new to me. I used to practice these Christian disciplines according to the way I had been taught and to what I had seen others doing. But the Holy Spirit wanted to teach me to worship according to the Word, to pray according to the Bible, to praise, to search, and to minister according to biblical patterns. I had to start reading the Bible to know God's heart. The Holy Spirit was prompting me to search the Scriptures through worship.

The apostle Peter went through the same experience. After three and a half years of listening to Jesus' words, he still didn't understand that the Messiah had to die, be placed in a tomb where He would remain for three days, and then rise from the dead. When, on the morning of Jesus' resurrection, Mary Magdalene saw that the stone at the entrance of the tomb where the Master had been placed had been removed, she went running to Peter. As soon as he heard the news, Peter rushed to the sepulcher. When he arrived, he went in and saw the strips of linen lying there, as well as the burial cloth that had been around Jesus' head folded up by itself, separate from the linen (John 20:1–7). It was evident Peter and the other disciples had not understood the Scriptures (John 20:9–10). That same night, something wonderful happened. Jesus came into the room where the disciples were gathered behind locked doors.

> Jesus came and stood among them and said, "Peace be with you!" After he said this, he showed them his hands and side. The disciples were overjoyed when they saw the Lord. Again Jesus said, "Peace be with you! As the Father has sent me, I am sending you." And with that he breathed on them and said, "Receive the Holy Spirit."
>
> —JOHN 20:19–22

Fifty days later on the Day of Pentecost, those same disciples who had not understood the Scriptures received the promise. Peter, filled with the Holy Spirit, preached a powerful message before a crowd of Jews. He quoted the prophecies of Joel and those of King David in Psalm 16 and Psalm 110, and he interpreted them in relationship to the coming of the Holy Spirit. What had transpired was that the Holy Spirit had touched and illuminated the Scriptures to him. From that point on, when the crowds of new believers gathered, "they devoted themselves to the apostles' teaching" (Acts 2:42).

What did the apostles teach? What Jesus had taught them. Who brought Jesus' words to their minds? The Holy Spirit. Who gave them the understanding to teach "doctrine"? The Holy Spirit.

HUNGER FOR THE WORD

AFTER THE HOLY SPIRIT had manifested His presence to me, I

161

felt a great hunger to understand my experience through the Word of God. In the beginning, the Holy Spirit led me to study the Psalms. King David knew God intimately. I always wanted to know God in the way David did, but I was more interested in studying the profound truths of Paul's epistles. The psalms, Moses' experiences in Sinai, Isaiah before the throne of God, Ezekiel, and John in the Book of Revelation had never attracted my attention. Actually, I would avoid studying those experiences, first because I didn't understand them, and second, because I felt reproved by them.

Notice carefully what I am saying. I had tried to know God intimately through a systematic study of the Bible. Now, the intimacy I had with God in prayer and adoration was leading me to study the Word afresh. I was drinking from Christ's presence first, and then that very presence was leading me to understand His Word.

One of the psalms that brought fresh revelation to me was Psalm 119, which is dedicated to the excellencies of the Word of God. It starts by saying:

> Blessed are they whose ways are blameless, who walk according to the law of the LORD. Blessed are they who keep his statutes and seek him with all their heart.
> —PSALM 119:1–2

Throughout this psalm, the writer talks about two things: obedience to God's Word and seeking Him with all our heart. The psalmist is placing himself in a position of worship before he receives God's Word, His direction, and His commandments. These are the steps he takes:

1. He seeks God.

"I seek you with all my heart" (v. 10). He wants to seek his God so he can be blessed and happy, and so he can keep and obey His commandments. There is no happiness with God without a search. There is no obedience to God without a relationship and without intimacy.

2. He humbles his heart before God.

"Turn my heart toward your statutes" (v. 36). The psalmist confesses that only God can incline his heart toward the Word. Humbling ourselves is not our tendency; our natural inclination is to do whatever we want to do. But in the presence of God, the Holy Spirit inclines our heart, our mind, and our will toward His Word. Jesus says it this way:

> If anyone loves me, he will obey my teaching. My Father will love him, and we will come to him and make our home with him.
>
> —JOHN 14:23

One cannot keep God's Word without loving Christ. Without a loving relationship with Jesus, you obey the Word because of fear or tradition. This type of religious obedience leads to frustration and confusion. When there is a loving relationship of worship and dependence on Him, there is renewal in the Word of God. The Word of God is no longer a technical manual; it is spirit and life.

I learned to prepare my heart and my mind to receive the revelation of the Word of God.

3. He asks for the revelation of the Spirit of the Word.

"I call with all my heart; answer me, O LORD, and I will obey your decrees" (v. 145). As a good Jew, David knew the demands of the divine law very well. The Law was very clear. He who violated it, committing acts contrary to what was established, was punished. Now David longed to obey God's laws out of a heart of obedience.

One day, Jesus was teaching about the Law. He said that

although the Law established what adultery was, if a man just looked at a woman lustfully he had already committed adultery with her in his heart. Jesus was teaching about the *spirit* of the Law, not the *letter*. To commit a homicide according to the Law, one had to murder somebody. But under the spirit of the Law, whenever we say something bad against a brother, we are committing murder.

4. David asks to understand the teaching or the ways of God's precepts.

"Let me understand the teaching of your precepts" (v. 27). What is a way? It is the direction one takes to reach a certain place. The ways of God are the directions, the steps we take toward Him. But notice that David was requesting understanding beyond obedience to the laws of God. David realized that God had a deeper revelation behind the Law of Moses. The Law ordered Israel to keep the Sabbath as the day of rest. During that day, nobody worked. But God's original intention was not simply that Israel not work one day a week. There was a "spirit," a "truth" behind this commandment. God wanted His people to learn to rest in Him, in His promises, and in His power. When we begin to learn the "ways" of God's demands, we don't learn the letter; we receive the revelation of the spirit of the Word. When we receive the spirit of the Word, the Bible says that we "have life." We receive God's life, which leads us to obedience and the fulfillment of His will without much effort on our part.

5. He implores the presence of his God.

"I have sought your face with all my heart" (v. 58). The psalmist recognizes that without the manifest presence of God, he can't keep the commandments. In the following verse, the psalmist says that after seeking God's presence with all his heart, he considered his ways, contemplated his life, and turned his steps to God's statutes (Ps. 119:59). What made him consider his ways? What made him turn his steps to God's statutes? The manifestation of the presence of God in his life. Intimate communion with his God.

6. He waits for God's answer.

"My soul faints with longing for your salvation, but I have put my hope in your word" (v. 81). When the heart asks for an answer, God responds according to His Word. The heart of David was waiting for God's instructions. This is a patient heart that knows already that human ideas lead to destruction. Only God's answer can save us.

7. He asks for understanding.

"May my cry come before you, O LORD; give me understanding according to your word" (v. 169). The psalmist asks for understanding after the answer has arrived. The heart of the psalmist not only expects an answer, but also the ability to understand it. Before the knowledge of the Word there has to be an intimate and open relationship with the God of the Word.

> Then you will know the truth, and the truth will set you free.
>
> —JOHN 8:32

The word *know* implies "to understand, to come to know something through personal experience." This knowledge has a beginning, a development, and a fulfillment. It isn't just an intellectual understanding. There is an experience. When the woman that had been subject to bleeding for twelve years reached and touched Jesus' cloak, she was instantly healed.

Immediately her bleeding stopped and she felt in her

body that she was freed from her suffering.

—MARK 5:29

The word translated as *felt* is the same word that is translated as *will know* in John 8:32. When the source of her bleeding dried up, this woman knew by personal experience in her body that she had been healed. She didn't know it by faith; she experienced it in her body. The truth of Christ, of His Word, and of His commandments has to be known in the same way this woman knew in her body that her bleeding had stopped.

Jesus knew the Father because He was one with the Father. The Father knew the Son because He was one with the Son, too. To know the truth is to be one with the truth. To know the truth is to experience it, to understand it, and to live it. The truth is neither a thing nor an idea. The truth is a person, and His name is Jesus. To know Jesus is to be one with His heart, His purposes, His person, and His life.

In Ephesians 1:18–19, the apostle Paul speaks about three blessings that we have received from the Father:

- "The hope to which he has called you" (v. 18).
- "The riches of his glorious inheritance in the saints" (v. 18).
- "His incomparably great power for us who believe. That power is like the working of his mighty strength" (v. 19).

These are glorious truths. We are called to *hope*. The word *hope* speaks about a firm expectation of good things. The believer in Christ is destined to overcome, not to be defeated. We are called to *riches*. Christ has secured an inheritance for us. One day in the heavens, we will receive it. In the meantime, the Father has given us His Holy Spirit as a deposit. Finally, we have received *power*. This power was demonstrated in Jesus' resurrection. We have the hope that a rich and glorious inheritance, together with the power that raised Jesus from the dead, is present in all the saints.

KNOWLEDGE VS. WISDOM

IN THE FIRST chapter of the Book of Ephesians, the writer tells us about the blessings we have in Christ in the heavenly places. But Paul knew that no matter how much he explained it to them, the Ephesians would not "know" these truths. He therefore prayed:

> I have not stopped giving thanks for you, remembering you in my prayers. I keep asking that the God of our Lord Jesus Christ, the glorious Father, may give you the Spirit of wisdom and revelation, so that you may know him better. I pray also that the eyes of your heart may be enlightened.
>
> —EPHESIANS 1:16–18

In verse 18, Paul talks about enlightened eyes. The believers in Ephesus had to be able to see the hope, the inheritance, and the power. We can see those things only when the Father gives us revelation and wisdom in the knowledge of Jesus the Son—not with human sight. Notice that the Father doesn't want to give us only revelation and wisdom. He wants to give us the "Spirit of wisdom and revelation, so that you may know him better" (v. 17). The Holy Spirit is the one who gives us this. But what is this Spirit of wisdom and revelation?

- *Wisdom* means "knowledge acquired through studying."
- *Revelation* means "the discovery of hidden truths; the manifestation, the appearance of something that was hidden."
- *Knowledge* means "to know through experience."

The Holy Spirit is the only one who gives us the ability to study the Bible, revealing to us the truths of the Word and leading us to experience the intimate knowledge of Jesus.

In my theological academic preparation and systematic study of the Bible, I obtained *wisdom*. But after my renewal, the Holy Spirit *revealed* truths to me that led me to the *knowledge* of Jesus, my King and my Lord.

Our main goal must be to know Christ, the Son of God. My goal is not simply to acquire biblical wisdom or knowledge of the Word. God wants to reveal His purposes for my life. What good is it to know the genealogies and the names of God and the apostles by heart if I don't know the will of God for my life? I don't want any theological knowledge if I'm not capable of having an intimate relationship with the Father. All this is the work of the Holy Spirit.

I, therefore, recommend the following steps:

1. Before studying the Word of God, worship Him.

Seek His presence. Honor Him with your lips and with your heart.

2. Surrender your mind and your heart to the Holy Spirit.

Cast aside all presumption, expectations, and traditions of the past. The Holy Spirit wants to teach you new things.

3. While you worship, have your Bible at hand, as well as a concordance and a Bible dictionary.

If the Holy Spirit puts a word or an expression in your heart during worship, look for it in the Bible and the concordance, and then look for the meaning of each word in the Bible dictionary.

4. Ask for revelation.

When studying the meaning of the words, ask the Holy Spirit to reveal to you what they mean for your life. We need to receive the revelation of the spirit of the Word.

5. While studying, don't forget that the Bible is Jesus' letter to you.

In the words of the Bible, Jesus is revealing His heart to you. He wants you to know Him. We need to search the Bible in order to have more intimacy with Jesus.

6. Be ready to change.

The Father will give you wisdom, revelation, and the knowledge of Christ, not so you will know, but so you will change. To know Christ is to be one with Him. The Holy Spirit speaks to us, leads us to a Bible passage, and reveals its meaning. The Spirit doesn't do it to give us biblical knowledge or so we can have a religious or mystical experience. The Holy Spirit does it because He knows that passage will free us from whatever is holding us in bondage, is stopping our growth, and is unpleasant to God. The Holy Spirit leads you to a Bible passage to change you. When the Holy Spirit transforms you, you know Christ.

> I want to know Christ and the power of his resurrection and the fellowship of sharing in his sufferings, becoming like him in his death.
> —PHILIPPIANS 3:10

Paul wanted to know Christ. We know Christ when we experience the power of the Resurrection. All that is dead in my life has to be resurrected. All that is worthless has to die and resurrect to new life. We know Christ when we share in His sufferings. The suffering of Christ found its culmination on the cross. The cross is where all our human efforts, our flesh, our wisdom, and our ego have to be placed also. This is how we will be transformed into His image—by suffering, crucifying all that is unpleasant to our

Father, and being resurrected as we surrender into the hands of the same Spirit that raised Christ from the dead.

The disciples were humble men, but they had been with Jesus. They had "become infected," not with intellectual knowledge but with spiritual knowledge of the Word of God. The anointing of Jesus changed those illiterate humble fishermen into experts in the Word.

Become infected with spiritual knowledge of the Word of God. Don't read just any Christian literature—read books written by people who show evidences of real and personal experiences with God. Read books of men and women who have been with God. These kind of books have led me to want to know and seek God more. They have motivated me not only to study the Bible, but also to know the God of the Bible. When these writers talk about God's truths and quote Bible passages, read these passages. You will see that the Holy Spirit will lead you into other passages, other Bible references. Use a study Bible. In it, you will find the definitions of the words and inspirational messages of men and women who have a deep experience of God. Many times the commentaries, definitions, and explanations of Bible passages have encouraged me to deepen my study and investigate a related topic.

Such study has led me to know and experience the will of my heavenly Father, the grace of the Lord Jesus Christ, and the communion of the Holy Spirit. Without this dimension, my knowledge is nothing but "dead letters." Without this dimension, I know the Word, the *logos,* but I haven't experienced the Word, the *rhema.* Faith comes from hearing the Word of God. Jesus said that man lives by every word—*rhema*—that comes from the mouth of God.

WORD OF CONSOLATION

Then Peter remembered the word Jesus had spoken.
—MATTHEW 26:75

Peter didn't remember what he had heard Jesus say. He didn't understand the Scriptures or the prophecies of the Old Testament about the things that were taking place. During the arrest, trial, crucifixion, and resurrection of Christ, he didn't remember the Scriptures. However, in the darkest and saddest moment of his life, he remembered the word, the *rhema,* of Jesus: "Before the rooster crows, you will disown me three times" (Matt. 26:34).

The word that Jesus had spoken to him was life. It had come from the mouth of God. When he heard it for the first time, Peter reacted emotionally. The aggressive disciple responded that he would never disown Jesus. But that word was deposited in Peter's heart without his realizing it. In the precise moment of the betrayal, the word came alive in his heart and produced tears of repentance. Those words of Jesus produced life and faith in Peter. He didn't cry because he felt bad; he cried because the word, the *(rhema)* confronted him with his betrayal. But he also remembered that after Jesus had spoken to him the word *(rhema)* of his failure, He had immediately pronounced a word *(rhema)* of consolation:

> Do not let your hearts be troubled. Trust in God; trust also in me.
>
> —JOHN 14:1

Many years later, this same Peter would declare these words:

> All men are like grass, and all their glory is like the flowers of the field; the grass withers and the flowers fall, but the word [*rhema*] of the Lord stands forever. And this is the word [the Good News] that was preached to you.
>
> —1 PETER 1:24–25

Eleven

THE MINISTRY:
THE FRAGRANCE OF CHRIST

THE LAST THING the Holy Spirit renewed in my life was my ministry. The Spirit of God started by changing my private spiritual life, and then He changed my public one.

The first letter to the Thessalonians, chapter 5, verses 23 and 24, talks about God as a God of peace:

> May God himself, the God of peace, sanctify you through and through. May your whole spirit, soul and body be kept blameless at the coming of our Lord Jesus Christ. The one who calls you is faithful and he will do it.

The peace between God and the believer is based entirely in the salvation performed and accomplished by Christ on our behalf. For that reason, God sanctifies, separates, and dedicates us for Himself, for His service, and for His glory. He sanctifies us. We can't sanctify ourselves.

The sanctification of the believer is not an option; it is a promise of God. He will separate us completely for Himself, for His service, for His honor, and for His perfect and absolute glory.

THE SANCTIFYING PLANS OF GOD

THE PASSAGE CONTINUES by saying that God will sanctify "our whole being." God promises to completely sanctify every aspect of our being: spirit, soul, and body. However, God doesn't sanctify us only in part. When God sanctifies, He renews our spirit, our soul, and our body entirely.

Whatever is changed in the spirit of man will have an impact upon his soul and will then affect the body. God wants to sanctify us so we can become instruments in His hands.

Why does He do it? First, because He is faithful, firm, secure, and He doesn't change. We can trust in Him. He does not sanctify us because we may be doing something that inspires confidence, but because He is sure His purposes will be fulfilled through our lives. Next, He does it because He calls us. Notice that the passage above expresses continuous action. God is continually calling us with a loud voice by name, and He promises to sanctify us completely and perfectly in spirit, soul, and body.

What God gradually started to do in my inner man was reflected in my external behavior. God started to completely renew my entire being. What was taking place in my devotional life, in my worship, and in my intimate relationship with God started to manifest at work, in my home, and in my relationship with others.

The ministry is a consequence of the work of God in our private spiritual life. Many think that taking a position in ministry will improve our intimate and private relationship with God. That isn't so. The ministry is only one fruit of our close and loving relationship with God. In that relationship, we receive the knowledge and the revelation of Jesus, we learn to recognize the voice of the Spirit, and we receive the riches of which we will then testify to others in the work of the ministry. Without that close relationship, we will have nothing of God to give.

In the second letter to the Corinthians, Paul illustrates

what a true ministry is like when it emerges from a close relationship with Christ. The apostle had received orders from the Holy Spirit to go to Macedonia, and he had made all the necessary arrangements for the trip except for a traveling companion. From his previous missionary journeys he knew he might face persecution, torture, and jail. Therefore he was hoping to go to Macedonia in the company of Titus, whom he calls "my brother." However, when he arrived at Troas, he didn't find Titus there. This is the way he described it:

> Furthermore, when I came to Troas to preach Christ's gospel, and a door was opened unto me of the Lord, I had no rest in my spirit, because I found not Titus my brother: but taking my leave of them, I went from thence into Macedonia.
>
> —2 CORINTHIANS 2:12–13, KJV

Because of his close relationship with God, the call to Macedonia had come to him through a vision. But suddenly he realized that he had to leave alone and with no peace in his spirit.

THE VICTORY IS SECURE

EVEN THOUGH HE had no peace in his spirit, Paul knew that he could depend on God, who would lead him in triumph, as he affirms in 2 Corinthians 2:14: "But thanks be to God, who always leads us in triumphal procession in Christ."

The expression "leads us in triumphal procession" was used in reference to the welcome received by the armies who had been victorious in war. The entire population of a town or region would come out to receive the soldiers who were returning from a military victory, carrying trophies, treasures, and booties. Paul declares that in spite of having to go alone, and knowing he would be persecuted, he could still give thanks to God in anticipation of the victory for the gospel that would be celebrated in Macedonia.

Notice that Paul explains that this victory celebration didn't just happen occasionally. God would *always* lead him to triumph, because "through us [God] spreads everywhere the fragrance of the knowledge of him" (2 Cor. 2:14).

In other words, Paul declares that every time and in every place where one of God's messengers goes, God manifests Himself through different channels to make visible what was invisible before—"the fragrance of the knowledge of him."

To welcome the armies that came back victorious from war, a city would prepare a very elaborate celebration. Most people would receive the soldiers with flowers and incense that scented the atmosphere of the celebration. As they approached the city, the soldiers knew by the fragrance of the flowers and incense, which could be perceived from a distance, that a celebration awaited their arrival. As they entered the city, the people would let out victory and welcome shouts. The aroma was a symbol of victory, an evidence of the fact that they had arrived home to their city, families, and to the reward they would receive for the victory achieved.

Paul explains that in the ministry, God uses us as channels to manifest the aroma of His knowledge so others can know Him. Only those who have been sent by God can be used as channels to manifest the aroma of the victory of Jesus Christ.

The Bible talks about the triumphal entry of Jesus Christ:

> Having canceled the written code, with its regulations, that was against us and that stood opposed to us; he took it away, nailing it to the cross. And having disarmed the powers and authorities, he made a public spectacle of them, triumphing over them by the cross.
> —COLOSSIANS 2:14–15

Christ had His triumphal entrance against sin, against the powers and authorities on the cross. Although we know very well our Savior suffered the cruelest death any human being can experience, those six hours of crucifixion were the triumphal victorious procession of Christ in His struggle against God's judgment caused by our sins. Christ made a public spectacle of the powers and authorities that enslaved us. When our sin was canceled on the cross, Christ was victorious—and so were we. The written deed of our crimes against God was canceled, taken away, and nailed to the cross. Our accusers, the devil and his powers, also had a written code against us. Christ took it away from them. Now there are no more accusations for those who are in Christ Jesus.

THE AROMA OF THE DIVINE PRESENCE

WHEN A MAN sent by God arrives at a place, the aroma of victory becomes evident. It is the aroma of Christ's triumph on the cross when He removed our guilt and sins and took back from the principalities all accusation that legally held us enslaved to the forces of darkness.

But there is something else. When the victorious soldiers would approach the city and smell the scent of the flowers, another group of people would be with them. Behind the victorious soldiers were the defeated ones, the slaves, condemned to prison or to death. The aroma that excited the victorious soldiers would terrorize the prisoners of war. For those who overcame, it proclaimed triumph, victory, and honor. For the prisoners, it meant jail, punishment, and death.

As a Latin American living in the United States, I am concerned by the indifference I perceive in many men and women of God toward satanic works in our nation. Many Christians seem to believe that satanic activity takes place only in Third World countries, in places of poverty, and in the occult world. For that reason, the church hasn't taken her spiritual authority in the war against hell. It is easier to organize a public march of protest than to organize a meeting of intercession. What makes us think we are exempt from the attacks and strategies of the devil? We must proclaim the decree of the cross, the victory of Christ, and the defeat of darkness, being always on alert, never ignoring our enemy. He never rests, and we shouldn't either.

When God manifests the aroma of Christ's victory on the cross, the enemy also perceives the aroma of his defeat. In the aroma of Christ, manifested through the ones who have been sent, God reveals Christ. Those who surround us know Christ, not because we convince them with colorful language or well-prepared arguments, but because the aroma of the victory of Christ makes known "in every place" the victorious Savior. "For we are to God the aroma of Christ among those who are being saved and those who are perishing. To the one we are the smell of death; to the other, the fragrance of life" (2 Cor. 2:15–16).

I once heard the story of a little bear who had lost his family. One of the bears from another clan adopted him as his protégé. In one of his expeditions, the cub was confronted with a lion that threatened to kill him. Suddenly, the lion became terrified and ran away. The little bear didn't realize that behind him stood the big gigantic bear who was protecting him. The lion wasn't afraid of the little bear; he ran away because he saw the larger bear behind the cub. The enemy will run from us when he sees Him who is within us—Jesus, the Son of God.

The lost are saved when Christ's aroma manifests through those who are sent by God to all places. The oppressed are set free from bondage when the decree of the cross is publicly declared. However, Paul wonders:

> And who is equal to such a task? Unlike so many, we do not peddle the word of God for profit. On the contrary, in Christ we speak before God with sincerity, like men sent from God.
>
> —2 CORINTHIANS 2:16–17

No one is sufficient to manifest that aroma. God is the

only One who makes it known. But here we see that God evidences it in the life of those who know they are not capable of manifesting it. Who, with sincerity, speak as men sent from God, before God, and in Christ. As ministers who desire to manifest the aroma of Christ, we must give attention to the following truths:

1. We must recognize our incompetence before the magnificence of our God.

Incompetent believers know they need His help. When God provides His protection, they triumph.

2. We must be sincere.

The adjective *sincere* applies to those things that even in daylight appear pure. Sincere is the person whose motivations and testimony shine because of that person's purity, even when subject to an intense scrutiny.

3. We must speak as men sent by God.

We are simple messengers. When the mailman comes to your house carrying a letter, you don't celebrate his arrival. You were not expecting him but the letter he was bringing. When you go to a restaurant, you don't celebrate the waiter but the dish he is serving. We are simply the mailmen who deliver the correspondence of the Good News to the world. We are the waiters who serve the delicious meal of the Bread of Life. The celebration, the honor, and the feast are for the One who sent the letter—Jesus. The feast is for the Bread of Life—Jesus.

4. We speak before God.

The ministry is carried out under God's scrutiny. This should incite in us a reverential fear. All we say, do, and think is done under the eyes of God. One day we will give an account of all we have done.

5. *We need to speak "in Christ."*

Paul describes what it means to speak in Christ.

- To speak in Christ is to speak of the New Covenant, the "gospel," not of the Old Covenant (2 Cor. 3:6).

- To speak in Christ is to speak of the ministry of the Holy Spirit, who is life, not of the law, which is death (vv. 6, 8).

- To speak in Christ is to speak of justification, not of condemnation (v. 9).

- To speak in Christ is to speak of freedom in the Spirit of the Lord (v. 17).

- To speak in Christ is to speak of the transformation of the believer into the likeness of Christ by the Holy Spirit (v. 18).

God promises that the aroma of Christ will emanate from us whenever and wherever we speak in this way. If we don't, we profit by falsifying the Word of God. To profit is to gain (*lucre*). The following characteristics can be found in those who peddle the Word of God:

- They brag about their talents and abilities.

- When exposed to the light, they do not reflect purity. The things they say do not confirm the way they live.

- They don't speak as men sent from God. They speak only about their own interests and human opinions.

- When they speak, they try to please others or to conform to the ideals and politics of others.

- They speak about obligations, burdens, yokes, legalisms, and external sacrifices, which must be fulfilled in order to be able to achieve God's favor. They do not speak about grace, the New Covenant, or the finished work of Jesus on the cross.

- They don't teach about the work of the Holy Spirit who transforms us from glory to glory. They teach transformation is achieved through human efforts and submission to ecclesiastical dogmas.

Those who corrupt the Word of God will always oppose those who want to spread the aroma of the knowledge of Christ. Paul reminds us of the following:

> For our light and momentary troubles are achieving for us an eternal glory that far outweighs them all. So we fix our eyes not on what is seen, but on what is unseen. For what is seen is temporary, but what is unseen is eternal.
>
> —2 CORINTHIANS 4:17–18

What a powerful truth! Those who have opposed my ministry do not dislike me or believe I'm doing things that are bad. Many just simply don't want to admit they need to be renewed, because renewal would require change. Their opposition, although painful, has produced a weight of glory in my life. If I would choose to resist, argue, or complain, I would be looking at "what is seen." When I choose to overlook the accusations and attacks, I fix my eyes on what is unseen, on what the Holy Spirit is doing. He is performing an invisible work in the heart of believers who are hungry, and He is producing a weight of glory that has nothing to do with what is seen. God is transforming His people because He wants to spread the aroma of Christ's victory on the cross.

In many places where the Word of God had been corrupted, the world perceived the stench of ecclesiastical structures. Thousands have gone into the world with the message of this church or that religious ideology. Thousands have gone out to spread the official doctrines of their organizations. Those who corrupt the Word of God cannot tolerate other ideologies, and they attack and criticize by bragging they are the only true speakers of God's revelation.

Those who spread Christ's aroma don't look at the temporal. They are too busy knowing Jesus. They are determined to know Christ in "the power of his resurrection and the fellowship of sharing in his sufferings, becoming like him in his death" (Phil. 3:10). They know the aroma of Jesus Christ flows out from a life that knows Him by experience, from a secret and private relationship with Him.

THE MINISTRY OF THE LEVITES

GOD SET THE members of the tribe of Levi apart to be His ministers, His servants:

> At that time the LORD set apart the tribe of Levi to carry the ark of the covenant of the LORD, to stand before the LORD to minister and to pronounce blessings in his name, as they still do today.
> —DEUTERONOMY 10:8

The Levites were instructed to carry the ark of the covenant upon their shoulders. The ark reminded them of the eternal covenant that the Lord had made with His people. Every time Israel would see the Levites carrying the ark, they would remember and celebrate the covenant God made with Abraham, which was confirmed through Moses. The ark was the visible manifestation of the covenant,

181

including the promise of the presence of the Lord in the midst of His people.

The Levites didn't have to utter one word; they just had to carry the ark as a remembrance of the covenant. In this way they exalted God and declared without words that He was with His people.

SERVANTS OF GOD

AS SERVANTS OF GOD, we don't carry the reminder of God's covenant with His people over us—we carry it in us. Our reminder is not an ark, but the deposit guaranteeing our inheritance, the Holy Spirit. He is the guarantee that we have been accepted in the Beloved, that the Father has accepted the sacrifice of Christ for us, and that we have eternal life. God's servants are instruments through which the Holy Spirit appears to comfort and edify the body.

Each servant is an ark. Each servant of God who walks through life is a living reminder of the covenant accomplished on the cross for eternal life. The Holy Spirit wants to manifest His power and His gifts through servants devoted to bring His manifestation to whomever is in need.

Each servant is called to stand before the Lord. The servants of God have been called to dwell and abide constantly before God. To *dwell* is "to establish a permanent residence." God's servants are called to dwell permanently in the manifest presence of God. This is exactly what Paul means when he declares, "We speak before God."

Each servant serves God. Servants abide in God's presence to serve Him. The Levites offered Him the sacrifices of animals and grain offerings. But "through Jesus, therefore, let us continually offer to God a sacrifice of praise—the fruit of lips that confess his name. And do not forget to do good and to share with others, for with such sacrifices God is pleased" (Heb. 13:15–16).

God's servants dwell in His presence praising, worshiping, doing good to others, and helping those in need. Every time we praise and worship our God for what He did in Christ, we offer a sacrifice. Every time we do what is good, what is correct, and what is just, we offer a sacrifice. Every time we help those in need, we offer a sacrifice and serve God.

The highest ministry of God's servant is not to preach, sing, or do good deeds for others to see. The Bible teaches us that the most excellent work is to minister to God. When we help those in need before men, we do it for others. But when we praise, do good, and help others, with no desire to be seen by men, we are ministering to God. We are offering a sacrifice to God.

A servant pronounces blessings in His master's name. The noblest responsibility of the servant is to bless others in the name of God. Blessing others is a fruit that grows from spending time in the presence of the Lord. Blessing others flows from a life of praise and worship to the Lord, from a life of communion with God. Blessing others flows from a life that does what is good and helps those in need. The servant of God blesses others just as Paul teaches that he has been blessed:

> Praise be to the God and Father of our Lord Jesus Christ, who has blessed us in the heavenly realms with every spiritual blessing in Christ.
>
> —EPHESIANS 1:3

THE BLESSINGS OF EPHESIANS

IN THE FIRST chapter of Ephesians, Paul teaches that the Father has blessed us in Christ Jesus. Let's take a look at these blessings.

- *He chose us before the creation of the world* (v. 4). To *choose* means "to call by name." He called us, knowing that one day we would accept Christ.

- *He chose us to be holy and blameless in His sight* (v. 4). Our purpose in life is to live lives that are set apart for God and without stain, for His honor and glory.

- *He predestined us to be adopted as His sons* (v. 5). In this particular context, to *predestine* is "to plan." He planned our lives so that we would be His children. In spite of our sin, God had everything planned so He could adopt us instead of condemn us.

- *He made us acceptable in the Beloved* (v. 6). The word translated as *acceptable* is translated many times as "highly favored." It appears in Luke 1:28, where it says: "The angel went to her and said, 'Greetings, you who are highly favored! The Lord is with you.'" The angel declares that Mary is highly favored, full of grace, surrounded by God's favor, and honored. Ephesians 1:6 says that those who are in Christ are as highly favored as was Mary. To be accepted in the Beloved means that the Father loves us with the same love He has for His Son, Jesus, and that He listens to our prayers with the same attention He gives to Jesus' prayers. Even though these truths seem hard to believe, the Father accepts us in the same way He accepts His Son.

- *We have redemption through His blood* (v. 7). It is an ongoing redemption. We can, at any time, ask for the forgiveness of our sins. It is a forgiveness that flows from the riches of His grace. It is an unmerited favor that God has granted us.

- *He made wisdom and understanding to superabound* (v. 8). The believer is the wisest and most intelligent person simply because he knows Christ Jesus and has received all spiritual blessing in the heavenly realms. We do not have earthly wisdom and understanding, but our wisdom shames the wise of this world. We have known the mystery of His will, which had been hidden. The mystery is that the Father would bring all things in heaven and on earth together under Christ, in whom the purpose of God was revealed.

- *We receive an inheritance, having been sealed with the Holy Spirit, the deposit guaranteeing such inheritance* (v. 14). We will one day take possession of the whole inheritance. The inheritance of the believer is the one the Father had prepared for Jesus. He has made us coheirs of His glorious inheritance. In the meantime, the Father has given us a deposit, a first installment of that patrimony. That deposit, that first fruit, is the person of the Holy Spirit, the Comforter.

God's servants have to declare this blessing granted by God to His people. Some are specialists in reminding us of all the threats and dangers. And yet, the servants of God are meant to bless the people in the name of Him who blessed us with all spiritual blessing. A ship reaches her destination when the crew perfectly knows the route and the harbor to which they're going.

Exalt Christ

When Christ is exalted and the fragrance of the victory of the cross is manifested, Satan flees, sicknesses disappear, sin is canceled, the blood of Christ cleanses, and even death is rebuked. I didn't learn this principle in a Bible institute or in seminary. This truth was learned in the intimacy of worship and communion with Jesus.

I learned that in moments of worship, the Holy Spirit transforms and changes us. In times of communion, the Holy Spirit forms Christ in us. In moments of worship, I surrender at the feet of my King, and the Holy Spirit fulfills the promise that our Savior left us:

> He will bring glory to me by taking from what is mine and making it known to you. All that belongs to the Father is mine. That is why I said the Spirit will take from what is mine and make it known to you.
>
> —JOHN 16:14–15

> I tell you the truth, my Father will give you whatever you ask in my name.
>
> —JOHN 16:23

Jesus said the Holy Spirit would take from what was His. The Spirit takes from all that the Father and Christ have, and He makes it known to us. The Spirit takes the spiritual blessings in Christ and declares them into my life. The Spirit takes all spiritual blessings (the seven blessings from Ephesians 1) and declares them into my life. We therefore have the privilege of asking the Father in the name of Jesus. When we ask the Father to bless us according to the blessings that are in Christ, the Holy Spirit declares them to us, and we receive them in our lives.

In each little moment that we set apart to worship and communicate with our God, the Holy Spirit declares to us all the blessings the Father has given to us in Christ. The Holy Spirit not only proclaims the blessing, but He also carries it out in our life. Thus, Paul wrote:

> For this reason I kneel before the Father, from whom his whole family in heaven and on earth derives its name. I pray that out of his glorious riches he may strengthen you with power through his Spirit in your inner being, so that Christ may dwell in your hearts through faith.
>
> —EPHESIANS 3:14–17

The Father wants to give us strength with power through the Spirit so that Christ may permanently establish Himself in our lives. When He establishes Himself, His kingdom and

His rule are established, His power is manifested, His glory shines, His peace abounds, and His love comforts us.

We wholeheartedly join the apostles' exclamation:

> Now to him who is able to do immeasurably more than all we ask or imagine, according to his power that is at work within us, to him be glory in the church and in Christ Jesus throughout all generations, for ever and ever! Amen.
>
> —EPHESIANS 3:20–21

A MINISTRY WITH POWER

PUBLIC MINISTRY IS the result of close communion with God. After Christ establishes Himself in our lives, the Holy Spirit will strengthen us, and the Father will give us power to minister that goes way beyond all we could achieve with our own prayers and understanding.

In our praise and worship services, we have learned the following:

All worship is to the Lord. All that we say and do is for the glory and honor of Jesus. All words, music, and activity have to glorify our Lord, just as if He were sitting physically on the platform to receive the honor. We throw away whatever does not accomplish this purpose. The most important thing in every ministry is glorifying and honoring the Lord.

The role of the minister is to lead the congregation to fix their eyes on Christ. Through the music, prayer, preaching, and testimonies, we lead those who listen to focus their faith in Jesus Christ, the author and perfecter of our faith. If we lead people's attention toward human talents, church ideologies, and emotional manipulation, we are filling the place that belongs exclusively to Christ with empty, temporary ideas that will never change hearts. Only men and women who have fixed their eyes on Christ can lead others to do the same.

When we fix our eyes on Christ and glorify His name, the

Holy Spirit takes from what is His, declares it, and manifests it in our lives. When a person who is sick or depressed comes into a place where he or she is encouraged to place his or her faith in Christ, forgetting about the problem, the Holy Spirit will minister to that person. Our duty is to lead people to put their faith in Christ.

When we witness to unbelievers, we guide them to trust in Jesus, the only Savior. The moment that a person receives Jesus by faith, he or she is saved. When we pray for a certain need, we lead the one in need to trust in Jesus, our provider. The moment that person deposits his or her burdens on Christ and confesses by faith that his or her circumstances are in the hands of the Lord, that person receives freedom and comfort.

When we declare the Word of God to a congregation or to a particular person, we are leading our listeners to trust in Christ's promises, the living Word. The moment those who receive the message believe that the word is for them, the promises are fulfilled in their lives.

The role of the minister is to "disappear," to diminish, so that Jesus may grow. The role of every servant of God is to lead people to Christ. We are servants and messengers. He is the message. The most important thing is the message. The messenger disappears once the message has been declared. As long as we are the focus of attention, Jesus will not come into focus, and the Holy Spirit will be grieved. When we stop focusing on ourselves and start glorifying Christ, the Holy Spirit rejoices and takes from what is Christ's and carries it out in our lives.

Many people talk about the anointing these days. The anointing is a gift from God. The anointing is the pouring out of God's grace on a life with the specific purpose of blessing others. It is the manifestation of the power of God for the fulfillment of a divine mission. When God sends us on a mission, He pours out His anointing over us to achieve the results He desires.

The presence of God and the anointing are two different

things. The presence of the Lord is given to the church and every believer through the person of the Holy Spirit who dwells in the life of every person who has been born again. The anointing is the power of the presence of God in our life. That power comes when God sends us on a mission in His name. His promise was: "But you will receive power when the Holy Spirit comes on you; and you will be my witnesses in Jerusalem, and in all Judea and Samaria, and to the ends of the earth" (Acts 1:8).

First comes the Holy Spirit, the presence of the victorious Christ in our lives. Then comes the power to be His witnesses to the ends of the earth. To be witnesses means to share what Christ represents in our lives. To be witnesses is to affirm that what Christ achieved will be a reality in the lives of those who listen. This can only be done when the Holy Spirit gives us power. We can't be witnesses without that power. The world will believe if Jesus' witnesses speak and demonstrate the reality of Christ with power and anointing.

The Book of Acts describes how a handful of men and women were able to evangelize their communities, cities, nations, and almost the entire known world through the anointing of the Holy Spirit.

How is this anointing received?

We can observe several things in the group of believers who received the anointing when, for the very first time, the Holy Spirit was poured out over the church.

- "They were all together in one place" (Acts 2:1).

The one hundred twenty went to the upper room to pray while waiting for the Holy Spirit to come. There is no anointing without prayer. And the anointing doesn't come because someone is praying for us—it comes only when we obey Christ's orders to longingly wait and pray that the Father will anoint us with power to be witnesses.

- "Peter stood up" (2:14).

Immediately after being filled with the Holy Spirit, the apostles had their first chance to witness. As a crowd of curious people gathered around them, Peter stood up with the eleven disciples and spoke. The same disciple who had denied Christ a few days earlier preached a message so powerful, so anointed, that the Bible says, "When the people heard this, they were cut to the heart and said to Peter and the other apostles, 'Brothers, what shall we do?'" (Acts 2:37).

- They spoke in Jesus Christ's name.

Peter replied, "Repent and be baptized, every one of you, in the name of Jesus Christ for the forgiveness of your sins. And you will receive the gift of the Holy Spirit."
—Acts 2:38

The anointing and power of the Holy Spirit become evident when we speak in the name of Jesus. To speak in the name of Jesus is to speak on His behalf and with His authority. We say what Christ says and do what He does. This is essential in anointed servants. We don't express our opinion or project our talents or personalities; we don't seek any honor. We exalt Christ in all our words and deeds.

- They were devoted to the body of Christ.

They devoted themselves to the apostles' teaching, to fellowship, to breaking of bread, and to prayer (Acts 2:42).

The anointing is sustained by constant obedience to the Word of God and by submission to the established authorities of the church. The anointing is maintained when there is a clear and honest relationship among the brothers and coworkers. The anointing is maintained when we are members of a local body of believers, a church where we celebrate together the Lord's Supper in obedience to the command to do it until He comes. Finally, the anointing is sustained by prayer.

> Everyone was filled with awe, and many wonders and miraculous signs were done by the apostles.
>
> —ACTS 2:43

These are the fruits produced by the anointing in the ministry of God's servants.

Twelve

THE LATTER GLORY

IN EPHESIANS 1:17–19, the apostle Paul prays: "I keep asking that the God of our Lord Jesus Christ, the glorious Father, may give you the Spirit of wisdom and revelation, so that you may know him better. I pray also that the eyes of your heart may be enlightened in order that you may know the hope to which he has called you, the riches of his glorious inheritance in the saints, and his incomparably great power for us who believe. That power is like the working of his mighty strength."

In the previous verses, Paul speaks of the revelation of God's purposes from before the creation of the world, revelation that he received directly from Jesus (Gal. 1:12). In Ephesians 3:8–10, he adds:

> Although I am less than the least of all God's people, this grace was given me: to preach to the Gentiles the unsearchable riches of Christ, and to make plain to everyone the administration of this mystery, which for ages past was kept hidden in God, who created all things. His intent was that now, through the church, the manifold wisdom of God should be made known to the rulers and authorities in the heavenly realms.

In chapter 11, we made a list of the seven blessings the Father gave us in Christ. These blessings produce "good works," which demonstrate the manifold wisdom of God to the rulers and authorities in the heavenly realms. These blessings are for the church, and the good deeds they lead to are carried out by the church. When we fulfill His eternal purposes, God is glorified and magnified before the church, the world, and the authorities in the heavenly realms, including both good angels and creatures of darkness.

This concept is glorious to us. God accomplishes His purposes here on earth exclusively through His church. He is sovereign and has chosen to do it this way. If you are part of the church of our Lord Jesus Christ, the Bible says that God will show His power, His wisdom, and His good works through your life. If you are the only believer in your family, at work, or in your neighborhood, God will accomplish His purpose exclusively through you. As Ephesians 2:10 says, "For we are God's workmanship, created in Christ Jesus to do good works, which God prepared in advance for us to do."

THE HOLY SPIRIT IN ACTION

THANK GOD FOR the thousands of men and women who through the centuries have devoted themselves to evangelizing our nations. Yet in these days, we are witnessing a change in the church. God Himself is placing a hunger for renewal in His people. Many are tired of the routine, traditions, and customs that have made the life of the church very dry and rigid. However, they're not looking for external changes—they want to be renewed inwardly. The same Holy Spirit who placed in Paul the desire to pray on behalf of the believers in Ephesus is placing a desire for change in the hearts of many believers. The Holy Spirit is revealing what is in the heart of the Father, all the spiritual blessings that He has prepared in Christ for His church.

This is the desire that God has put in my heart and in the

heart of His people. We want to receive the Spirit of wisdom and revelation in the knowledge of Christ. Let us not be satisfied with the knowledge of God only through the things others have taught us. When we talk about ministry, worship, praise, and prayer, we are usually referring to activities that take place during a service at church. It is time for Christ to be known in every aspect of our lives. The Holy Spirit wants to show us the manifold wisdom of God at all times and in every aspect of our lives. The Holy Spirit wants us to understand that everything we do needs to be done with the wisdom and understanding of God. In the Book of the Acts, most of the miracles were not performed in the midst of the congregation of believers. More than 90 percent of them were performed in the work place, in the market place, in the main square.

Some time ago, I met a young girl, very devoted to the Lord, whose job was to clean houses. She told me she had recently fasted for twenty-one days. I asked her if she was too weak physically to handle her job. She answered that while she was fasting, the Holy Spirit showed her how to clean the houses, even how to handle the heavy buckets of water. I was impressed. In her job, even in her friendships, she had received God's wisdom. The Holy Spirit also gave her directions about to whom to witness, for whom to pray, with whom to develop a friendship, and even where to be able to get the best deals to buy clothes. This girl does not have a high position in the church. She simply cleans houses and is very happy doing it.

The Holy Spirit is active all over the earth. The whole earth is full of His glory. But to fulfill God's purposes here on earth, He needs an instrument to carry out the good works He has prepared for us. We are the only ones who can declare to the world that we have been saved by grace.

On the Sabbath, Jesus went into the synagogue and stood up to read. The priests handed Him the scroll of the prophet Isaiah:

Unrolling it, he found the place where it is written:
"The Spirit of the Lord is on me, because he has
anointed me to preach good news to the poor. He has
sent me to proclaim freedom for the prisoners and
recovery of sight for the blind, to release the
oppressed, to proclaim the year of the Lord's favor."

—LUKE 4:17–19

There are many people who talk about bad things, but
Jesus Christ came to announce the Good News in this way.
When He quoted Isaiah 61:1–2, Jesus didn't mention the
phrase "the day of vengeance of our God." That day will be
at His Second Coming. Now is the time to talk about the
year of the Lord's favor, the Year of Jubilee. The law of the
Old Covenant had established that every fifty years all debts
had to be canceled and every slave had to be set free
without exception. Jesus was saying the Word was being
fulfilled right at that moment. God has set us apart to proclaim, live, testify, and experience that same Word with our
lips and with our actions.

We want to see and experience the riches of Christ's glorious inheritance in the saints. Everything that God wants to
give us we have already. We already possess all the riches
and glorious inheritance of Christ "in the saints." You may ask:
"Where is it?" For this reason, Paul prayed for the believers in
Ephesus, not only so they could understand it intellectually,
but so they could experience it in their daily lives.

What is Christ's inheritance?

That power is like the working of his mighty strength,
which he exerted in Christ when he raised him from
the dead and seated him at his right hand in the heavenly realms, far above all rule and authority, power
and dominion, and every title that can be given, not
only in the present age but also in the one to come.
And God placed all things under his feet and
appointed him to be head over everything for the

church, which is his body, the fullness of him who fills
everything in every way.

—EPHESIANS 1:19–23

Christ's inheritance includes:

- Victory over death.
- A place at the right hand of the Father.
- Supreme authority over every name and power in the
  heavenly realms, on earth, and under the earth for-
  ever.
- All things placed under His feet.
- Christ's headship of the church.
- The church's role as His body.
- The church filled with the fullness of Christ on earth.

Christ has filled us not only with experiences; He has
filled us with Himself. This is also our inheritance. We have
victory over death. We are seated at the right hand of the
Father, which is a position of supreme authority. Although
we don't possess our own authority, we have been given
authority to use the name that is above all names, the name
of Jesus.

The disciples had an interesting experience exercising the
authority of Christ in their lives.

The seventy-two returned with joy and said, "Lord,
even the demons submit to us in your name."

He replied, "I saw Satan fall like lightning from
heaven. I have given you authority to trample on
snakes and scorpions and to overcome all the power
of the enemy; nothing will harm you. However, do not
rejoice that the spirits submit to you, but rejoice that
your names are written in heaven."

—LUKE 10:17–20

Notice that demonic spirits submit to those who have

been sent by Jesus. All things are placed under the feet of Christ. He is the head, and between the head and the feet is the church, the body. All things are then submitted to the church. The church is not a denomination, a structure, or a temple. The church is *you*—every person who has been born again of the Holy Spirit. Her enemies—the devil and his whole army—are already defeated.

I'm amazed at the experiences of evangelist Carlos Annacondia; his simplicity and humility impress me. When he talks about the work of the devil or the operation of demons and demonic sects, he does so in a very secure and quiet manner, as if he were talking about something very clear and simple. One is impacted by the spiritual authority of this man of God as one sees the demonic manifestations that take place simply because he begins to pray or simply because he comes into a place.

Do you know why Carlos Annacondia is different? Because he has received understanding and a vision of the authority we all have. Jesus didn't give any more authority to him than to you. The difference is that Carlos Annacondia sees it, understands it, uses it, and lives it. Great men and women of God are people who, while recognizing their own inadequacy, have a true vision of who they are in Christ. Their eyes have been enlightened to see the riches of the call upon their lives.

We want to see the mighty strength of the power of God, the same that was exerted in Christ's tomb when God raised Him from the dead and seated Him at His right hand in the heavenly realms.

The same Holy Spirit who revived the dead body of Jesus, raising Him through the heavens to sit at the right hand of the Father, dwells in us. That same Spirit will one day manifest His great power to transform us, glorifying our bodies from corruptible to incorruptible, taking us in the twinkling of an eye to the Lord's presence (Rom. 8:11). That Spirit will not descend on us in the Rapture, because He already dwells in us.

What do we have to do so that the power of the Spirit may manifest in us? What do we have to do so that the Spirit—the deposit, the guarantee of our inheritance—may work in us? What do we have to do so that the blessings given to us may become real and visible in our lives? The answer is found in the Book of Romans:

> Therefore, brothers, we have an obligation—but it is not to the sinful nature, to live according to it. For if you live according to the sinful nature, you will die; but if by the Spirit you put to death the misdeeds of the body, you will live, because those who are led by the Spirit of God are sons of God. For you did not receive a spirit that makes you a slave again to fear, but you received the Spirit of sonship. And by him we cry, "Abba, Father." The Spirit himself testifies with our spirit that we are God's children. Now if we are children, then we are heirs—heirs of God and co-heirs with Christ, if indeed we share in his sufferings in order that we may also share in his glory.
> —ROMANS 8:12–17

Simply put: Let's live according to the Spirit and not according to the flesh. In Galatians 5, Paul teaches us the Holy Spirit produces fruit in our lives. However, he also teaches that the flesh evidences works such as the following:

- *Adultery.* Illicit sexual relationships with a married person.
- *Sexual immorality.* Sexual relationships outside of marriage.
- *Impurity.* Moral impurity, private, secret, or public.
- *Debauchery.* Vices, sexual addictions, pagan, or worldly habits.
- *Idolatry.* To honor anything usurping the place that belongs only to God.

- *Witchcraft*. Occult practice that may include the use of drugs.
- *Hatred*. Animosities, personal feuds, unresolved disagreements.
- *Discord*. Quarreling, competition.
- *Jealousy*. Fear of being displaced.
- *Fits of rage*. Violent emotions, explosive rage.
- *Selfish ambition*. Conflicts. Partisan spirit.
- *Dissension or divisions*. The word *division* is made of two words: *di*, which means "two," and *vision*, which means "eyesight." Division occurs when two people who are supposed to see eye to eye cannot agree, and they separate.
- *Heresy*. Errors in matters of belief.
- *Envy*. Pain at seeing that others have what we don't have.
- *Homicide*. The taking of another's life. Galatians 5:15 speaks about believers who bite and devour each other. Paul says, "Watch out or you will be destroyed by each other." The tongue is many times more destructive than a firearm.
- *Drunkenness*. Numbing of the senses because of alcohol ingestion.
- *Orgies*. Immoral parties, out of control.

The Bible doesn't tell us to eliminate the natural inclinations of the flesh; it tells us not to satisfy the desires of the flesh. The secret to the crucifixion of the flesh is that the flesh must be crucified continuously. We must constantly offer our bodies as a living sacrifice. When we don't satisfy the desires of the flesh, the Holy Spirit will work in our lives so that the works of the flesh will die. So then, let's walk in the Spirit, not satisfying the desires of the flesh, but rather depending constantly on Him.

Walking in the Spirit is not a party; it is a battle between the Spirit and the flesh. He who walks daily in the Spirit will see the constant manifestation of the power of God in his life. He who satisfies the desires of the flesh will sow in the flesh, will reap corruption, and will not see the manifestation of spiritual blessings in his life. He who sows in the Spirit will reap the manifestation of the blessings of the Father according to Ephesians 1, and he will know the hope of His calling, the abundant riches of His inheritance, and His incomparably great power for him who believes.

God has called us to fulfill this purpose through our lives. Don't wait for God to do it through someone else. You are God's workmanship, created for the implementation of His plans. We are called to walk in the Spirit, bind principalities and powers in the name of Jesus, and demonstrate the manifold wisdom of God to all of creation.

Many God-fearing Christians who want to please God have developed "Christian" routines that become boring and repetitive. Many never see the manifestation of the blessings the Bible has declared belong to the believer. The most common error in the lives of believers is not the commission of the grossest sins. We are so careful not to fall into sins like adultery, fornication, witchcraft, drunkenness, and orgies. Yet we fail to avoid sins like jealousy, pride, dissension, and discord.

Many believers try to please God by praying, worshiping, praising, studying the Bible, and serving Him in the strength of the flesh. We ignore the fact that one of our most powerful enemies is the routine of self-motivated religion. The routine negates any attempted changes. It leads us to conformity—everything is done according to what has been determined beforehand, and nothing changes. This works well in a cemetery where everything is routine. In a cemetery, the dead will always be in the same place, and those who celebrate the rituals will always do it the same way. But this is not what God desires. This is not the Holy Spirit's will.

This is the secret of renewal—walking in the Spirit in every aspect of our lives, not only in our moral lives or our public behavior, but also in our "inner being." Our relationship with God can be corrupted and reduced to certain behaviors, conducts, and traditions, which, no matter how impressive they may be, will steal our vitality and renewal in the Spirit.

Watch how this works in real life. In our flesh there is the inclination to compete. Competition surfaces when we think our group, party, or family is better than others. This inclination, inherited from Adam, is a part of the sinful nature. In our Christian lives, we have applied this spirit of competition and denominational attitudes to the disciplines we have already discussed in this book. Historically we have seen how many Christian communities have given into competitions, convincing themselves that their biblical interpretations, their way of ministering, their way of praying, and their style of praise and worship are the correct ones, the ones that please God. This attitude has led many to criticize and even condemn other communities that serve God in a different way. It has also led many to even oppose the very term *renewal*.

A dear pastor from Argentina who had been part of the Renewal Movement in the seventies explained to me that some people who had participated in the movement were opposed to current-day renewal. They think that when they received the renewal in the past, they received it all, without exception. These people are not walking in the Spirit. They have an inclination to factions and divisions. Some even brag that they are "conserving" what they received many years ago.

They received the renewal corresponding to their generation. But today there is a new and fresh renewal for all who want it. Christ wants to reveal Himself again and in a different way.

After the death of the Lord on the cross, the disciples returned to their previous tasks. They had forgotten that when Jesus found them fishing the first time, He told them from that moment on they would not catch fish—but men. The disciples went back to depending on their own efforts to find sustenance. Jesus sought them out, found them by the sea, and without getting upset or finding it necessary to reprimand them, He called out to them, "Friends, haven't you any fish?" (John 21:5).

In some translations, Jesus calls them "little children." This is a term of endearment that an adult would use to speak to a child. The disciples probably thought the person calling to them was an old fisherman of the region. Jesus simply asked them if their human efforts had produced any fruit. The disciples answered that even though they were fishermen by profession and experience, they had had no success.

We won't have success either if we go back to the place we were when Christ first found us. Jesus' disciples didn't recognize the new and different manifestation of His presence. Then Jesus, the loving Teacher, told them to throw their net on the right side of the boat. When they did, a miracle occurred: The net was full of fish. They recognized this manifestation. They had seen the Lord showing Himself like that before. The first time they encountered Jesus, they had received the same miracle of catching a large number of fish. (See Luke 5:1–11.) When they saw a manifestation known to them, they realized it was Jesus.

There are disciples of Jesus today who still have this same tendency to step into the past. They think Christ will show Himself today in the same way He did yesterday. Many expect revivals to be the same as books describe the revivals of the past. But the Holy Spirit will breathe a powerful revival over the church with manifestations never seen before. God is the God of the new. God doesn't repeat Himself.

The account of what happened next to the disciples is well known: "When they landed, they saw a fire of burning coals with fish on it, and some bread. . . . Jesus said to them, 'Come and have breakfast.' None of the disciples dared ask him, 'Who are you?' They knew it was the Lord" (John 21:9, 12).

RENEWAL ACCORDING TO GOD

THE BELIEVER WHO is renewed recognizes his weaknesses. Our human ability tries to know Christ and to please and serve God. We try to analyze and organize Christ's manifestations of the past. But the only way to know Him is through the work of the Holy Spirit, who renews our understanding in the knowledge of Him. It is necessary to know that our flesh will fight against the Spirit, who wants to renew us in the knowledge of Christ every day. He wants to reveal to us new aspects of our calling, of the riches of our inheritance, of the power of God, and of our authority as children of the Father, the body of Christ, and His church. We, therefore, recognize as believers that we cannot please God with our own efforts or our best intentions. Those efforts have to be crucified, and we have to surrender so that the Holy Spirit may produce "fruit" in us.

The inheritance in us, the person of the Holy Spirit, produces in us the following:

- *Love.* The ability to give without expecting a reward or remuneration.
- *Joy.* A profound security in the midst of difficulties and trials.
- *Peace.* Quietness and tranquility in relationship with God and others.
- *Patience.* The ability to suffer, even for a long time, and to wait for the solution.
- *Kindness.* Sweetness of speech, gentleness.
- *Goodness.* Generosity; desire to do good.
- *Faithfulness.* To be consistent, sure, and reliable.
- *Gentleness.* Before hurting, allowing others to hurt us.
- *Self-control.* Control of one's temperament.

In the letter to the Romans, Paul teaches us that the riches, wisdom, and knowledge of God are deep. His judgments are unsearchable; they can't be analyzed. His ways are beyond tracing out; they can't be investigated. The apostle says, "For from him and through him and to him are all things" (Rom. 11:36).

In the next chapter, Paul concludes:

> Therefore, I urge you, brothers, in view of God's mercy, to offer your bodies as living sacrifices, holy and pleasing to God—this is your spiritual act of worship. Do not conform any longer to the pattern of this world, but be transformed by the renewing of your mind. Then you will be able to test and approve what God's will is—his good, pleasing and perfect will.
>
> For by the grace given me I say to every one of you: Do not think of yourself more highly than you ought, but rather think of yourself with sober judgment, in accordance with the measure of faith God has given you.
>
> —ROMANS 12:1–3

After recognizing our carnal inclinations, and after trying to please God through our own human efforts, comes the next step. My desire was merely *what not to be*—I did not want to be like the world. I wasted all my energies in not being "worldly." In the letter to the Colossians, Paul exhorts us to get rid of the old self. As soon as we are converted, we are immediately exhorted to leave our old practices behind. But this is only half of our Christian life. The second half concerns *what we are to be*. Paul teaches us to clothe ourselves with the Lord Jesus Christ, with our new self.

In Romans 12, we are exhorted to be transformed by the renewing of our mind. The word *transformation* in Greek is *metamorphosis*. This describes the process of a worm becoming a butterfly. How are we transformed? By the renewing of our mind and by the renewing of the knowledge and experience of Christ. Then we will be able to test and approve the will of God.

Have you ever asked yourself what the will of God is in

your life? I don't mean God's will for daily experiences, but rather His purpose for your entire life. The apostle defines it this way:

> What is more, I consider everything a loss compared to the surpassing greatness of knowing Christ Jesus my Lord, for whose sake I have lost all things. I consider them rubbish, that I may gain Christ.... I want to know Christ and the power of his resurrection and the fellowship of sharing in his sufferings, becoming like him in his death.... Brothers, I do not consider myself yet to have taken hold of it. But one thing I do: Forgetting what is behind and straining toward what is ahead, I press on toward the goal to win the prize for which God has called me heavenward in Christ Jesus.
> —PHILIPPIANS 3:8, 10, 13–14

Paul describes the purpose of God in his life as a "goal." This goal is a prize, the supreme calling of God, which is "in Christ" and is "to win Christ" by becoming like Him. In the letter to the Galatians, he explains it like this:

> My dear children, for whom I am again in the pains of childbirth until Christ is formed in you.
> —GALATIANS 4:19

That is God's purpose in our lives. The Holy Spirit dwells in our lives so that Christ Jesus may be formed in us. The Holy Spirit will transform us into the image and likeness of Jesus, having us go through the experience of death, pain, and total dependency on our Father. During those experiences of humiliation, personal loss, spiritual poverty, and total dependence on our Father, we are going to learn to be like Jesus. But as it happened to me, this experience always ends in the manifestation of the power of the Resurrection. God will exalt us and lift our heads. Then we will be able to experience the words of the apostle Paul:

> Your attitude should be the same as that of Christ
> Jesus: Who...made himself nothing, taking the very
> nature of a servant...and being found in appearance
> as a man, he humbled himself and became obedient to
> death—even death on a cross. Therefore God exalted
> him to the highest place.
>
> —PHILIPPIANS 2:5, 7–9

God's purpose is that we may become like His Son,
Jesus, the author and perfecter of our faith. What is
renewal? It is the ongoing work of the Holy Spirit, which
transforms us to become increasingly like Jesus.

> Put to death, therefore, whatever belongs to your
> earthly nature....You have taken off your old self with
> its practices and have put on the new self, which is
> being renewed in knowledge in the image of its
> Creator. Here there is no Greek or Jew, circumcised or
> uncircumcised, barbarian, Scythian, slave or free, but
> Christ is all, and is in all.
>
> —COLOSSIANS 3:5, 9–11

Yes, we have received all spiritual blessing in the heavenly realms in Christ. We have put on the new self. But this
is simply the beginning. There are still attitudes and carnal
reasoning—earthly ones—present. The believer who is
renewed dies to the earthly in his life and is renewed to the
heavenly so that Christ may be all in his life. As Christians
we can worship, praise, pray, study the Scriptures, and
even serve God with earthly motivations. Renewal doesn't
mean to change old habits for new ones. Renewal takes
place when:

- We seek for things above, where Christ is.
- We set our eyes on things above, not on earthly things.
- We die to things of this world.
- We are renewed according to the image of Jesus.

In worship, we discern the person of the Father and His wonderful plan for us to become like His Son. In worship, we contemplate the glory of God in Christ, evidenced in His love and in His grace. We contemplate the glorious "image," the beautiful "appearance" of Jesus. This process has no end. We will always be worshiping God, discerning who He is. Heaven will be a constant and eternal revelation of God.

In worship, we discern the victory and the security of His promises, which are *yes* and *amen* in Christ. This is an ongoing process. The more trials there are, the more worship there will be.

In prayer, we discern the desires and purpose of God in our lives. In prayer, we ask and receive the transformation, the changing into His image. This will be a constant process while on earth. When we get to heaven, we won't need to be changed because we will have already been changed "in the twinkling of an eye." Heaven is the complete fulfillment of God's purposes.

In studying the Word of God, we discern His voice; the enlightened Word is a lamp for our daily living. The Bible isn't simply a book or a text; it is the revelation of a person, and His name is Jesus Christ, the Son of God. When we arrive at heaven, we will be in the glorious presence of the living Word, the Alpha and the Omega.

In our service, we discern that we are God's channels to bless others. In the ministry, we are a blessing according to the life and power of Christ in us. It's not us, but the inner transformation the Holy Spirit has done in us that manifests to benefit others. This process will go on as long as we are surrounded by needs and those in need. When we get to heaven, the Lord will wipe away every tear, and there will be no need for us to minister to one another.

THE LATTER GLORY

PRAISE AND WORSHIP are the only two activities that will never cease. God is leading His people to a daily spiritual renewal. I'm not talking about the renewal of certain activities or disciplines. I'm talking about the renewal of our understanding in the knowledge of Him. There may be some who think they don't need to know Christ more than they already do—they have already received all knowledge and all revelation. God doesn't want us to adopt this attitude. In the Old Testament, He offered an invitation of renewal to His people, the Israelites, who had adopted a proud and vain attitude.

> This is what the LORD says, he who made the earth, the LORD who formed it and established it—the LORD is his name.
> —JEREMIAH 33:2

Before exhorting His people to renewal, the Lord reminded them that He is eternal, almighty, and omniscient. Man is extremely limited in his knowledge of God.

> Call to me and I will answer you and tell you great and unsearchable things you do not know....I will bring health and healing to it [the city of God]; I will heal my people and will let them enjoy abundant peace and security. I will bring Judah and Israel back from captivity and will rebuild them as they were before.
> —JEREMIAH 33:3, 6–7

God will not only bring back the wounded, those who have gone astray, and the exiled, but He will also heal them and give them back peace and truth, restoring them as they were before.

> Then this city will bring me renown, joy, praise and honor before all nations on earth that hear of all the good things I do for it; and they will be in awe and will tremble at the abundant prosperity and peace I provide for it.
> —JEREMIAH 33:9

This work of God in His people will be seen and heard by all. The nations will tremble, not because of God's judgment, but because of His great mercy and the great miracles He will perform on earth through His people.

> "There will be heard once more the sounds of joy and gladness, the voices of bride and bridegroom, and the voices of those who bring thank offerings to the house of the LORD, saying, 'Give thanks to the LORD Almighty, for the LORD is good; his loves endures forever.' For I will restore the fortunes of the land as they were before," says the LORD.
> —JEREMIAH 33:10–11

The voice of the believers will change. The music of the church will change. No more laments or expressions of pain or uncertainty will be heard. God will change our voices of sadness into voices of happiness and joy. The church will declare to the whole world that God is worthy of praise, because Satan had to return all he had stolen and all the souls he had held in prison. When the whole world is deserted and the streets are desolated, the believers are going to be the only ones rejoicing.

> This is what the LORD Almighty says: "In this place, desolate and without men or animals—in all its towns there will again be pastures for shepherds to rest their flocks...flocks will again pass under the hand of the one who counts them," says the LORD.
> —JEREMIAH 33:12–13

In days of economic crisis, believers will be the only ones with abundance in their homes.

> "The days are coming," declares the LORD, "when I will fulfill the gracious promise I made to the house of Israel and to the house of Judah. 'In those days and at

that time I will make a righteous Branch sprout from David's line; he will do what is just and right in the land.'"

—JEREMIAH 33:14–15

God promises to confirm the gracious promise, not a negative one of calamity. This promise will be confirmed when the Son of David appears—the One who renews, whose name is Jesus, from the house of Israel, from the tribe of Judah. The gracious promise that God has spoken from the beginning will be confirmed in the house of the righteous Branch, the church of the Lord Jesus Christ.

> This is what the LORD Almighty says: "In a little while I will once more shake the heavens and the earth, the sea and the dry land. I will shake all nations, and the desired of all nations will come, and I will fill this house with glory," says the LORD Almighty. "The silver is mine, and the gold is mine," declares the LORD Almighty. "The glory of this present house will be greater than the glory of the former house," says the LORD Almighty. "And in this place I will grant peace," declares the LORD Almighty.

—HAGGAI 2:6–9

The glory that will come over the church before Christ returns will be greater than the former. The former glory was poured out over the church in the upper room on the Day of Pentecost. The latter glory will be greater than on the Day of Pentecost. At Pentecost, Peter explained that with the outpouring of the Spirit on all people, the prophet Joel's word was being fulfilled, which also spoke about the early and the latter rain. The early rain descends before the sowing season. The latter one descends before the harvest, several months after the sowing, when the fields are white and ready for harvest.

Be glad, O people of Zion, rejoice in the LORD your God, for he has given you the autumn rains in righteousness. He sends you abundant showers, both autumn and spring rains, as before. The threshing floors will be filled with grain; the vats will overflow with new wine and oil. I will repay you for the years the locusts have eaten—the great locust and the young locust, the other locusts and the locust swarm—my great army that I sent among you.

—JOEL 2:23–25

In that day, the mountains will drip new wine, and the hills will flow with milk; all the ravines of Judah will run with water. A fountain will flow out of the LORD's house.

—JOEL 3:18

The latter glory will be manifested over the church, which was born in the upper room, at the time of the early rain. There is where the harvest was sown. Days of great harvest are coming to the church as we've never seen before. The early rain and the latter rain will descend together. That means we will sow and reap at the same time. That's why the Bible says the mountains will drip new wine. There will be no need to wait for the fruit to ripen. As soon as the seed is sown, it will ripen and be harvested immediately. Why? Because there will be a fountain in the church, and rivers from that same fountain of water will flow into the life of every believer, waters from the early and latter rain descending from heaven.

This flow does not occur simply so we can rejoice. It flows to create expectations, so that from now on we may start to praise our God. It is a declaration to principalities, to the world, to our friends who have already heard the testimony of salvation, and to our loved ones who still haven't accepted Christ. Their day of salvation is coming. You will be the one who sows and the one who reaps.

RENEW ME

After all this, the Lord will come to take up His own. The church will not leave this earth defeated and weak, but rather glorious and renewed. This promise is not just for an elect group of super Christians. This promise is for you! God will fulfill His purpose and His will through your life and mine.

Thirteen

OPEN HEAVENS

A FTER ALL I have said, I want to conclude with a truth that has transformed my heart. When in the previous chapters I said Jesus was our model, the Holy Spirit was forming Christ in us, and the life of Jesus would manifest itself in our being, do not take these truths as clichés. God has established that what He did in His Son, He will do in us.

> It was he who gave some to be apostles, some to be prophets, some to be evangelists, and some to be pastors and teachers, to prepare God's people for works of service, so that the body of Christ may be built up until we all reach unity in the faith and in the knowledge of the Son of God and become mature, attaining to the whole measure of the fullness of Christ.
> —EPHESIANS 4:11–13

In this passage, Paul teaches us that Christ, after His death, resurrection, and ascension, gave gifts to the church. These gifts are the fivefold ministries. They enable the saints, the believers, to find their proper place in ministry so they can build up the body of Christ. This process will last

213

until all of us, without exception, become mature. The mature Christian is like Jesus, having attained to the same measure, the same stature, and the same fullness of Christ. What a promise! The question is, Are we mature? The answer is no, not yet. So, what is then going to happen?

In Isaiah 7:14, God the Father declares that Jesus, His Son, would be a sign. "Therefore the LORD himself will give you a sign: The virgin will be with child and will give birth to a son, and will call him Immanuel."

Isaiah 8:18 says, "Here am I, and the children the LORD has given me. We are signs and symbols in Israel from the LORD Almighty, who dwells on Mount Zion." In this passage, God declares that not only was Jesus a sign, but also the children whom God had given Him would be a sign. What is a sign? What does a sign do? A sign points out. A sign directs us on the path that will lead us to our final destination. When we go to the airport to catch a flight to another city, we first have to go to the check-in desk to receive an authorization to be on that flight.

When we arrive at the check-in desk, we search for the correct flight to take us to our final destination. We look for a sign. But when we find the sign of our flight, we can't just stand there in front of the sign, thinking we have reached our final destination. We are just standing in front of the sign. To reach our final destination we must complete the journey.

Jesus was the sign. Jesus was pointing to someone who would come after Him as the fulfillment of His work. Jesus was pointing to us, His children, the mature who would come after Him. To become mature, we have to complete the journey of renewal. Allow me to show you that journey.

How was Jesus born? He was born of the Spirit. How were you born? You were also born of the Holy Spirit. When Jesus was conceived by the Spirit, He was pointing to us. In the same way He was conceived by the Holy Spirit, we were born of the Spirit too.

A few days after Jesus was born, Herod tried to kill Him.

A few days after our new birth, Satan also rises up to kill and destroy us. The same evil spirit that attempted to kill Jesus is still trying to destroy all the Spirit conceives. Don't be confused if all hell has risen against your life. Jesus is our sign. We will have to go through the same experiences He went through in His life.

An angel told Joseph to escape to Egypt. Mary, Joseph, and the child (the sign) left Israel to go to Egypt. In the Bible, Egypt always represents sin, the world, and captivity. There they stayed for two years. After achieving the first victories in our Christian lives, we have to face our past, our old friendships, old vices, and old ways of living. Jesus was indicating to us the way. We also have to face our "Egypt," our slavery that doesn't automatically disappear when we accept Christ. Don't be discouraged if you are in the middle of this process.

After Egypt, Joseph, Mary, and the child Jesus returned to Nazareth. The Bible doesn't say much about these years in Nazareth. One thing we know: Jesus went back to Nazareth to grow up. After His deliverance from Herod, His victory against Egypt, Jesus returned to His hometown to grow in grace and strength and to be filled with wisdom (Luke 2:40). On our path to become "mature," we have to grow up.

We don't know much about Jesus' childhood, but when He was twelve years old, we find Him in the Temple. Many say He was conversing with the teachers of the Law. The Bible says that Jesus did two things: He listened, and He asked questions. (See Luke 2:46.) Luke also says that everyone who heard Him was amazed at His understanding and His answers (v. 47).

Jesus had been growing physically. He couldn't confront the teachers of the Law as a baby. He waited until He was twelve. At thirteen, Jewish boys are declared men. Jesus, with a lot of respect and grace, left everyone amazed. Jesus was pointing out the path of our Christian life. We have to grow in strength, grace, and wisdom also.

After this experience, we don't know anything about the years of His youth. Joseph, Mary, and the young Jesus went back to Nazareth. Jesus didn't start His ministry yet. Jesus went back to work in the carpenter's workshop of His father, Joseph. He learned to clean, to sweep the shop's floors, and to build furniture. He learned to work, submitting to Joseph's supervision. Jesus was pointing out the way to us. We have to work in the things of the Lord. We have to start by working at the most humble and menial jobs. Jesus did it, and we have to do it, too. Jesus worked as a carpenter until He turned thirty. He didn't rush into the ministry. His day was still to come.

Suddenly a peculiar character enters the scene. He was John the Baptist, the son of a minister and a minister himself. But he never preached in his father's church. He wasn't like other ministers—he dressed differently, had a different diet, and his message was quiet and strong. It was based on Isaiah's message, which is found in Isaiah 40. John came to announce the coming of the kingdom of God, the coming of the Anointed One, the arrival of the promised Messiah. John the Baptist was preaching with the anointing of the spirit of prophecy.

Before God does anything here on earth, He sends the spirit of prophecy. The prophets are, in most cases, a little strange; they are not like everybody else. We've never heard a stronger prophetic voice over the church than we are hearing today. Everywhere, the spirit of prophecy is announcing the last great revival visitation over the earth. The prophets are proclaiming that we must prepare the way for the manifestation of the glory of God. The prophets are shouting at the top of their voices that we have to repent; the church of Jesus has to repent of her sins, her pride, and her religiosity.

Many have doubts; others are criticizing the prophets because they are weird. Others don't want to go where the spirit of prophecy is manifesting with signs and evidences of the glorious explosive manifestation of the majesty of

God. Many tell me it isn't necessary to attend crusades led by anointed men or to go to cities where churches are experiencing a revival. They say that if God wants to touch them, He can do it wherever they are. But the people in John the Baptist's days went to the desert to listen to him. Jesus went to the desert by the Jordan River to be baptized.

But one day... There is always *one day* in God. One day the Father's appointed time arrived. Let me tell you this: Your day will come too. You may have been waiting for a long time. Jesus waited from the time He was thirteen until He turned thirty. In the meantime, He worked with His father, Joseph. In God's appointed time, Jesus went to the Jordan River to be baptized by John. Jesus yielded to the Father's will when He submitted to the spirit of prophecy in John. Let us submit to the spirit of prophecy, which is announcing first the great visitation over the church and then over the whole earth. Jesus, our sign, yielded and fulfilled the will of His Father.

In God's time, heaven opened, and two things happened.

The Holy Spirit came upon Jesus in a visible, tangible way. It wasn't just a simple manifestation; the Holy Spirit rested on Him and never left again. The Holy Spirit filled Him completely with His person and anointed Him under open heavens.

The Father spoke and declared that Jesus was His Son. But that wasn't all. He was His Son, and the Father was well pleased with Him.

When the heavens open, the Holy Spirit manifests Himself visibly, and the Father declares His pleasure in His children. From that place, Jesus, our sign, was led into the desert. But don't forget! Jesus was led into the desert to be tempted by the devil under open heavens. What a difference that makes! Jesus came into the desert to defeat Satan!

From that time on, Jesus walked His three and a half years of ministry on earth under open heavens. There was no interference in the communication between the Son, the Father, and the Holy Spirit. Whatever the Father would say or do, Jesus said and did. The Father said and did in the heavens, Jesus declared it on earth, and the Holy Spirit accomplished it, anointing it to make it evident.

Satan continued tempting Him. Religious people would not leave Him alone, constantly setting traps to try to ridicule Him. The trials, the disappointments, and the rejections didn't disappear. But in the midst of it all, Jesus walked under open heavens.

Before returning to His Father, Jesus instructed His disciples to stay in Jerusalem to wait for the Father's promise. Jesus was telling them that what He had received in the Jordan River, they would receive in the upper room—open heavens. And when the Day of Pentecost came, the day appointed for the one hundred twenty, the heavens were opened. The Holy Spirit manifested Himself visibly, not as a dove but as tongues of fire. A violent wind blew and they all started to speak in other tongues. When Peter went out to the street, he preached a message, and three thousand people were converted that day. These are the results when there are open heavens.

The church went to preach under open heavens. The people of that day tried to stop the church, but angels defended her, took the believers out of jail, and saved them from shipwrecks. Even Jesus' healing virtue manifested itself in Peter's shadow. The Book of Acts ends by saying that the gospel was preached "boldly and without hindrance." In the last book of the Bible, God opens the heavens and reveals the plan of the ages to the church.

Dear reader, I know this book has awakened in you a hunger for more of God. You will have to go through times of confusion and frustration as you wait for the Spirit's intervention in your life. Probably you have desired that someone with a great anointing from God would impart a portion of God's glory to you. Allow me to tell you that is a good frustration. Hunger is good. It allows us to know that we are healthy and our digestive and nervous systems are functioning well. One of the first evidences of sickness is loss of appetite. If you are hungry and frustrated because you want more of God, glory to God!

This is my advice:

- Follow the example of our sign, Jesus.
- Allow God to cleanse you from all ties to your old way of living.
- Grow in the knowledge of the Bible. Read books that will help you grow.
- Work at your church. Don't look for positions of notoriety. Do whatever your authorities order you to do. Devote yourself to being obedient and submissive.
- Listen to every prophetic word the Lord gives you, and keep it. Don't rush into anything. Keep on working.
- Believe what the spirit of prophecy is saying about the greatest revival on earth. Believe, and you will be a part of it.

Your day will come. God will take you to the right place. He will place you in the exact spot so the heavens may open and He can promote you.

Don't be afraid of trials; they are opportunities to defeat Satan.

Be faithful unto death as the early church was, not seeking any recognition, riches, or position. The glory belongs to Jesus Christ, our Lord.

ABOUT THE AUTHOR

Born and raised in Rosario, Argentina, David Greco has lived in New York and New Jersey since 1971. He is an ordained minister with the Spanish Eastern District of the Assemblies of God. In addition to serving as executive director of Radio Vision Cristiana since 1984, he ministers on the air via the program *Momentos de adorar* (*Time to Worship*). The program, now shared by other ministers at the station throughout the week, is an open-ended period of prayer, worship, and Bible study. The format of holding extended devotional time before an open microphone grew directly out of his personal renewal experience.

Outside the station, he ministers in churches throughout the New York City metropolitan area and in conferences and crusades throughout Latin America. He also serves as a Bible teacher at Calvary Temple in Wayne, New Jersey, where he attends with his wife, Denise, and their three children: Anafaye, Christi, and David.

ABOUT RADIO VISION CRISTIANA

Radio Vision Cristiana is a network of listener-supported radio stations that cover the New York City metropolitan area, the Caribbean, and parts of Central and South America. Radio Vision is heard over 1330 AM in New York City; 530 AM in South Caicos, Turks, and Caicos British West Indies; and 1330 AM in Santo Domingo, Domican Republic.

Radio Vision's headquarters are in Paterson, New Jersey. The programming, most of which is live, is handled by New York City metropolitan ministers representing a cross section of denominations and nationalities. The prophetic and evangelistic message being forged in the Hispanic church of New York City is delivered twenty-four hours a day via satellite to the ministry's international audience, which includes a strong following in Communist-controlled Cuba.

If you would like to contact the author,
you may write or e-mail him
(in either English or Spanish)
at the following address:

DAVID GRECO
P. O. Box 320674
Brooklyn, NY 11232
E-mail: davidgreco@compuserve.com